A Man of Two Worlds

Memoirs by Anesti Nova

Relating the experiences of a Christian, born and raised in the cosmopolitan era of Istanbul.

His observations relating to the causes of the downfall of that society.

Relating his immigration to America as an accordionist and music teacher, but facing the changing circumstances of music to Rock and Roll.

Relating how he became a popular restaurateur, and how his predictions for a future "Saddam Hussein" political affair came true, and the red flag of Yemen".

Experiencing the unexpected death of the spouse, and how through his psychic research discovered the "Power of love."

Sharing his responses to the 9/11 tragedy, the emergence of protective angels, and his inspirations for musical compositions, which he believes came from God.

BookLocker.com, Inc.
2010

Acknowledgments

Professor Lamont Thomas who encouraged me to write my life story, wanting me to call it, "An Old Wolf Looks Back."

Professor Dr. Michael Gates who was my mentor in writing this book. He patiently and enthusiastically listed to the experiences of my life.

My Yankee wife, Elizabeth Norris Lotreck Nova, who was my unofficial editor—since English is not my first language—and who gave me the "space" needed for compiling my memoirs.

In addition I am grateful to Lamont, Michael and Betty and the many other people who have inspired me in my life's journey.

Each immigrant to America has his or her own story.

TABLE OF CONTENTS

INTRODUCTION

As I think about writing my memories, my mind goes in many directions, because my life has so many scenarios interwoven with many cultures.

1938 was the year when Atatürk died at the age of 57. As a war hero, he was able to kick out the Sultan and establish the new Republic, Türkiye. He reformed Turkish culture by separating the State from Religion for the first time in a Muslim country. Atatürk also made it possible for Europeans who had fled Communism to live together in Istanbul in peace and safety. These were the times when my father, like other Christian immigrants, decided to make his home in this most beautiful city of Istanbul.

I was born in 1935 and raised in Istanbul as a Turkish citizen. My parents were Albanians and members of the Greek Orthodox Church, believing that the Patriarch (the head of the Christian Orthodoxy of Constantinople, now Istanbul) would be their protector should the political situation in Turkey change.

My father first experienced Istanbul when he was a young boy. It was during the Ottoman Empire and people could move freely from one country to another in the Balkans, which in the early 1900s included Greece, Albania, Bulgaria, Yugoslavia, Hungary and Romania.

When my grandfather brought my father to Istanbul, then the capital of the Ottoman Empire, he had the idea that a young boy should learn a trade *and* other languages. Schooling was not considered as important as knowing a trade; consequently, my father received little formal education, but this did not stop him from becoming a successful businessman, as well as a self-educated leader in three cultures: Albanian, Greek and Turkish.

1

When he decided to marry and raise a family, he contacted his relatives in Albania to see if a match could be made. They sent him a picture of my mother. On seeing that picture, my father decided to invite her to Istanbul in 1921. When they met, it took no time at all for my father to decide to marry her. The simple wedding ceremony took place within a few days. The marriage happened so quickly that my father did not have time to make arrangements for their living quarters. They spent their first night together in a relative's house. In our culture at that time, couples did not date or spend time getting to know each other! Obviously, my mother did not have a choice in the final decision.

CHAPTER I: My Childhood

My parents had six children, but the first two died in early childhood. My mother was superstitious and when the third child was born, my brother, she took him to the intersection where two streets crossed and placed him there in the road, believing that if he were saved by a passerby he would survive. She then watched from the side of the street waiting for the first person to approach the baby and asked him to name her son. Startled by this request, after collecting his thoughts, the passerby named him (Panayot), which is Peter in English.

Superstition of the age also included the piercing of one ear of the baby to wear a small earring. Peter wore that till he was old enough to realize men did not wear earrings. Now he is an active 80-year-old, dividing his time between Chicago and Florida. After Peter, my mother had two daughters and then me. My mother never repeated her superstitious act. Maybe it worked just for him, or did it carry over to us as well?

My mother was a typical Albanian wife who took care of the household chores, while my father worked in a Turkish style restaurant in Istanbul. He gave my mother money to cover the household expenses, and she was able to pay the bills and even save a portion of it. They were the symbol of the Albanian philosophy which says: *We have two hands, one golden and one silver—which one is golden and which one is silver?* The answer—The one that saves is golden, and the one that earns is silver! You can imagine who had the gold and the silver hand in my family.

They moved to a small wooden house perched on the edge of a small cliff, where a brook ran along the bottom. This cliff was a constant worry for my mother. My older sister remembers playing near the cliff and losing three balls on three occasions, all of which rolled over the edge. Of course, the cliff was too steep to recover them.

She remembers also, our mother leaving me (I was three or four years old) in the living room with my older brother who was doing his homework. There was a wood-burning stove in the room and I was playing around it, when I put some newspapers in the stove which ignited immediately. Startled, I knew I should not have done this. I quickly took the flaming paper out of the stove, which began smoldering on the oriental carpet. My brother was so engrossed in his reading that he did not react to the smoke! It was my mother who came to the rescue, putting out the fire and scolding my older brother for being inattentive to his baby brother.

I had a yellow hunter cat who kept away the mice and other rodents. When our family grew, my father bought a new concrete house in the next town.

I remember in our move to our new house I was upset because my cat wouldn't come with me. Obviously, he was territorial and wouldn't budge!

I even went back to the old house later to find her and give her comfort. But when I tried to carry her away, she would jump and run back to the old house. She must be like territorial humans who won't move (emigrate) to a new land—like my uncle who died in a communist prison.

The new house had two stories. We lived on the second floor because it had more room. The first floor lost much of its living space because the laundry was located under the stairway, where there were two large stone sinks used by my mother—one to soak and the other to rinse the clothes. Later she got a rickety washing machine that vibrated so much it looked like it was dancing! My job was to turn the hand-controlled ringer to squeeze the wash water from the wet clothes. Laundry day was busy and tough for my mother.

We started using a stove that burned coal, as well as a Coleman stove that burned kerosene. As a result, our home was no longer filled with dust, dirt and smoke from the old wood stoves.

**Nostalgic steam train taking people
from the city to suburbs**

SUMMER VACATION IN FLORYA

I remember as a child riding in a wagon drawn by two horses as my father's worker was moving our household possessions from the city of Istanbul to the countryside. This trip was a two-hour wagon ride to Florya, where my father rented for the summer a farmhouse close to a sandy beach.

I loved those horses that pulled my father's wagon. They were like a husband-wife team. When one was not in a good mood, the other one pulled more and vice versa. It was like sharing the burden of life. My father used them to pull the wagon to deliver specialty meats from the slaughterhouse to his restaurants around the city. In 1948 he replaced the horses with a small truck.

During sunny days we used to take the horse and buggy from the farmhouse to the beach, where I had to cover my mother in her one-piece bathing suit with hot sand because she had arthritis in her legs. Her doctor suggested that she stay as long as she could in the hot sand as therapy to ease the discomfort. For almost an hour she had the patience to endure the hot sand and sun. Her body was covered with perspiration. Afterward enduring this therapy, she would run to the refreshing sea for relief and to wash off the sand. She did this therapy several summers. (Sadly, this beautiful town of Florya is now occupied by housing for a million people. What was once an idyllic countryside is now an overgrown polluted little city.)

Because we had no running water, as I grew older, I was assigned another task, which was to carry water using two jugs from the fountain down the street to our house, My relatives gave me the nickname "Saka," which is Turkish, for *the waterman*. When an aunt made fun of me, I dumped the water in her entryway. I don't remember what the punishment was, but another aunt told my mother that the other aunt deserved it. Eventually I became *Pashaj i nenose,* which means, "favored son" in Albanian.

Life during the summer was so natural, in Florya. Even though I was a city boy, I enjoyed the work on the farm. One of the tasks was threshing the wheat. Before we had threshing machines, the Turkish farmers used strong wooden boards with broken pebbles stuck in the board in a fixed position so the sharp side could be against the wheat. When the horse was pulling the board, I would stand or sit on it to give it more weight. The threshing was completed after a few rounds for that load.

We enjoyed fresh milk from the cows, but I was told to stay away from the bulls after one of our cousins was gored. The eggs on that farm were so fresh in the morning that they were still warm when we would eat them raw with a little salt, or when whipped with powdered sugar to a foamy consistency like an eggnog—very delicious to eat. We did not worry about cholesterol then.

I loved to watch those lovely yellow chicks follow the mother hen. One day I wanted to caress one of them. My mother jumped to protect me from the hen, yelling, "You dare not touch the chicks because the mother hen will pluck your eyes out!"

The roosters were colorful, and later when we rented an island house, I had my own rooster as a pet. I enjoyed him waking me up early in the mornings crowing *cock-a-doodle-do*! And then there came a time when my mother decided to cook him for dinner. I was so upset that I did not eat for a day.

Because my father wanted us to have the best education, we attended very good schools in Istanbul during the cosmopolitan era of the 1930's.

THE PRIVATE GREEK SCHOOL AND THE CORSICAN BROTHER

We all started education in the private Greek elementary school of Feriköy, one of the toughest schools with six grades. Besides Greek and Turkish, we had to study French in fourth grade and ancient Greek in the sixth grade! Like all the private schools in Istanbul, we also had a class in the Greek Orthodox religion. A point of interest was that the Turkish government required all the private schools to have classes in the official Turkish language. We also learned about Atatürk's revolutionary reforms, which included a secular government and his insistence that people should leave their personal beliefs at home and in their houses of worship. He mandated a dress code which forbade any display of religious garments in the street, including the garb of the Muslim clerics!

My father was a benevolent trustee in that community. With his comrades he rebuilt both the school of "Feriköy" and the church that was called The Twelve Apostles.

7 : Τὸ Νέον Σχολικὸν Μέγαρον

9 : 'Η Α. Θ. Π. ὁ Οἰκουμενικὸς Πατριάρχης 'Αθηναγόρας
μετὰ τοῦ Α. Συμβουλίου τῆς Κοινότητος

**Ecumenical Patriarch Athenagoras congratulating my
father and his comrades for rebuilding the
school and Church**

In school we had a dress code and we experienced harsh discipline for infractions. Even the janitor had the right to punish naughty students with a stick. But one day when I was punished, the pain of the stick made me so angry that I grabbed it and broke it into pieces. I had the support of other students who cheered me on because they also had felt the stick!

As a result, the principal stopped the janitor from using the stick for punishment, realizing the time had come for that type of punishment to end. That was the beginning of my becoming a *dissenter*.

I am happy also, that I had the instinct to protect my classmate Niko from the bullies who picked on him because of his effeminate actions. He used to describe me as his Corsican brother (from Alexander Dumas).

My older sister barely finished the school, but my younger sister went on to a French high school, *Notre Dame de Sion*. When I was sent to pick up my sister at the school, I loved to listen to the nuns playing: Bach, Handel and Frank on the Organ.

TRADITION

My father, as in old generations, had a basic theory about raising sons. He believed that the son who was very good in school should be sent to College. The son who did not do very well should go to a technical school or learn his father's business.

My older brother was the smartest. He skipped first grade and later he graduated as the youngest student from the American Robert College (Boğaziçi) and he earned a scholarship to Purdue University. He worked for International Harvester as a mechanical engineer. When he returned to Istanbul to marry, he was required to serve in the Turkish military as a reserve officer. He was assigned to NATO to build an army ordinance 5th echelon factory, train Turkish soldiers, and undertake the preparation of M-36 and M-24 tanks as well as anti-aircraft guns for delivery to the Turkish armies.

My brother Peter as a reserve Turkish officer

When his reserve service was terminated, he was delayed from discharge until his replacement—an army colonel—was acquainted with the various services of military army ordinance! When he returned to Istanbul as a civilian, he decided to initiate entrepreneurial enterprises. He founded a new factory that used German machinery and a conveyor system for a new product, the first of its kind to become a success.

13

But the Cyprus affair became a political football. A popular non-Muslim factory became a target. In the demonstrations of September 6-7, 1955, the factory was completely destroyed! So, he realized he had to leave Turkey for good. Luckily his old boss needed him in International Harvester, which is now Navistar. As a technology immigrant, he became a promoter of computer technologies and one of the top ten computer experts to undertake systems computer design for six Fortune 500 companies. He also used the Pentagon system of Internet design before the Internet became a popular commercial product. By the time he retired, he owned his own company specializing in advanced computer systems.

In comparison to my brother, I was not a good student. I neglected my homework because I found those assignments boring and I was overloaded with three languages.

My mind was on music and soccer. So, my father decided I should not go to college, which was a mistake according to my brother, who knew how good I was at learning the English language.

My father, on the basis of the principle of his work ethic, wanted me to work for somebody else for two years. He arranged an apprenticeship with a jewelry maker in order for me to learn the work ethic. I learned to make some simple crosses and chains, which were made into charm bracelets. I also learned to create wedding rings, etc.

THE ROAD TO BECOME A TURKISH STYLE RESTAURATEUR

Then, I started working with my father—first to learn the trade in buying and handling the specialty meats in the slaughterhouse, and secondly, to learn the restaurant business as a waiter, and then a cook. Eventually, I became a boss.

I worked in the slaughterhouse four days a week. Owned by the city, it was located in the outskirts, at the end of the seawater inlet named Golden Horn, in Turkish, that would be called *Haliç*. There were five large buildings, the first one for cows and bulls. The cows and calves were a big job to handle, but the most dangerous job was handling the bulls. They were brought in early in the morning and chained to the ground. Sometimes when they smelled the blood they would go wild and break the chains and run to kill! The people in the building had no other choice than to shoot the bull carefully. Even my father had a gun.

The second building was for the sheep and lambs. The third building was for restaurant owners like my father who, with their workers, cleaned and skinned the specialty meats to be ready for delivery. The fourth building was the steam room and the fifth was for hogs. All the buildings were connected with rails and hand driven carts to move the specialty meats.

The specialty meats included cow stomachs and feet, sheep stomachs, lamb intestines, livers and heads.

The cow stomachs had to be delivered with carts to the dock next to the building where a barge was available to take the waste of the stomachs and cut off the sections called *omasum* and *abomasum* (stomach parts), which were cleaned separately. They would then turn the rest of the stomach (tripe) inside out wash them with seawater pumped from the inlet and send to the steam room where the dark side of the tripe was taken off. These were then turn inside out again and skinned off that side of the tripe with a skillful knife technique. The lamb intestines were cut off with a special razor-sharp knife, its edge covered with lead.

I was trained in the first weeks as carefully as a surgeon. A professional person was assigned to me to hold me when I fainted on seeing the blood!

Ranchers and businesses would sometimes pay the city for the services of their skilled butchers to handle the carcasses, to skin off-jobs, take out the intestines, stomachs and steam room jobs, etc.

Working in the slaughterhouse

Thursdays I worked in the restaurant with my uncle Michael, my father's best partner, who was a tough man to work for. He trained me with discipline to be a waiter and a cook; I learned how to handle and chop up the tripe next to a big kettle, which was heated and boiled 24 hours a day with logs we would cut from the forest. From my uncle I learned that the trees on the east side of the mountain were more expensive, because the trees on the east side absorb more sunshine, and they burn better. Eventually the log-fueled ovens were replaced with gas. One special oven, which in Turkish is called a *Tandır*, was fired up with wood charcoal with a small opening on top. It was tough to control the burning of the charcoal and the smoke that burned your eyes, while at the same time baking the mutton, lamb heads, specialty of lamb intestines stuffed with liver, kidney, and hearts as kebobs.

TRADITIONAL TECHNIQUE FOR HIRING A WORKER

My uncle would walk two or three miles from his house before 5:00 am to the restaurant, which he would open at 6:00 a.m. and close at 3:00 p.m., working six days a week with no vacation. His unique method of hiring a worker was this: After asking his name and age, he would tell him to sit down and have a bowl of tripe soup on the house. Then he would turn back to his workbench, but observe this young man to see if he would consume the soup in a slow inattentive manner, or if he would be like a hard worker who would consume the soup quickly and then thank my uncle. That was the test to get the job!

In my free time I studied English in night school, I also learned the Telegram-Morse Code and was certified to be an international telegraphist. My dream was to travel with big ships. Because the rules regulating international shipping changed, they were not hiring younger people any more to train them. I had to abandon that dream, though by that time I was only sixteen.

I then decided to work with my father and in my free time to concentrate on music, swimming and chess until I would be drafted into the military.

Johann Strauss (the king of waltzes) made me start in music and I wanted the violin, but my father did not like the squeaky violin, so I had to start with my brother's accordion and with the top accordion instructor of the country, Pandeli Citra, who used to order the latest top accordion compositions from Europe and America for his students.

My uniform for International Telegram operator

**A ferryboat dwarfed by the carrier as it took
people to the islands of Marmara**

CHAPTER II: Johnnie

Johnnie was the nickname given American sailors in Istanbul in the 1950s when I was fifteen. After World War II, Istanbul and Dardanelles became the key to the Mediterranean Sea. Turkey preferred to side with America against the old enemy, Russia, who became a godless country with Communism. At those times the Turks wanted to persuade their own people that Christians and Americans believe to the same God, which brings them together against the godless (*Allahsız*) country. Eventually, it was General Marshall's plan that made the relationship stronger between Turkey and America.

So the U.S. Navy docked in the port of Istanbul, and made its presence felt in the town of Karaköy (port area of Istanbul) where my father had his Turkish style restaurant.

American sailors flocked to the city from the visiting warships of the 6th Fleet. I remember commuting in the summer on the ferryboat between the restaurant and the island where we had our summer home. As the ferryboat would pass by the huge carrier, I could not help but wonder how the Americans were able to put a mountain on the sea!

My father built a steady clientele for his business in the Turkish restaurant. His specialty, made in a big kettle, was tripe soup. It was loved by all Turkish and Balkan people, and was said to be especially beneficial for the customers with hangovers because tripe soup has the highest amount of pepsin.

Also, my father specialized in kebobs, tandir kebobs—which were better than shish kebobs—the special meats were baked in built-up special stove using wood charcoal. My father and his three partners owned four restaurants around the city.

The busiest location was the one closest to the port, and our neighbors used to send the sailors or any tourists to me for directions or questions if they spoke only English. Mondays seemed to be especially busy!

Through the years, I tried to help the Johnnies to find their way to the main street—Beyoğlu—where the bars and nightclubs were, helping them find entertainment and relief from military duty. In my young age I felt affection for those clean, neatly-dressed sailors and officers who were friendly, ready to help other cultures, and who were always negotiating, bringing help, and giving us their business.

The presence of the U.S. Navy was a big attraction to everybody, but the Turkish girls were not like the Italian or French girls because they were from Muslim heritage and any flirting could be risky to their lives. The U.S. Navy personnel were attracted to the "Belly dancers," to the point that it became a fad, but it also caused trouble for the American wives and fiancées back home. Many of these American women had to learn belly dancing to keep their men happy!

Because of that fad, many Turkish belly dancers came to New York and other big cities to open dance studios!

One day one of the visiting U.S. Navy officers wanted to know what a Turkish style restaurant was. So I explained to him everything, also about the history of this location, that my knowledge came from a 95-year-old customer who told me that this restaurant had served people good food in the time of the "Sultans." He remembered how one of the Sultans would smell the food—when he was passing by on his horse to go to his palace (Dolmabahçe Sarayi)—and sent his servant to get his meal! That was the reason the restaurant was named *Meşhur Karaköy Işkembecisi* in Turkish, the famous Karaköy restaurant.

On one side, the narrow street had an underground well, called *Ayazma* in Turkish, and in Greek, Αγιαζμα, which means *Holy Water*. This water was drawn with a lift pump operated by the hand for the public. The name of that street was *Tulumba sokak,* which means *The Lift Pump Street.* I always intended to fix that lift-up pump for the public, because older people would tell me: *This water heals the eye sores.* They would also give me the Turkish blessing, *Allah senden razı olsun,* which means, "God bless you." I used to receive that blessing constantly every day till I left the restaurant and Istanbul, because every poor hungry man would get a soup on the house. My mother used to comment on my generosity by saying, "My son will never get rich!"

In response to my mother, I am reminded of the Turkish proverb: *Kiminin parası, kiminin duası,* which means, *Some people are happy and strong because they have money, and some people are happy and strong because they have blessings.* The latter part of this proverb may not satisfy those who consider money as prime goal of life.

One U.S. Naval officer was impressed with the story and he was surprised to see the size of the kettle—45 inches in diameter and 40 inches deep—sitting in the firebox, simmering constantly with the logs burning underneath. He was interested in tasting some kebob meat of the lamb head baked in the wood charcoal oven. So I ordered my cook to make a plate, but not to add any brain or eyes, but apparently he forgot. The officer loved the taste of the meat, but suddenly he stopped eating when he saw two eyes looking at him! He jumped up telling me that he can't eat any more, holding his eyes and showing his plate with the meat. I think that was an earlier and Turkish version of the Indiana Jones experience!

During those years I was also impressed with the visit of battleship *Missouri* and the music the sailors and visiting musicians brought with them—the jazz and blues of Louis Armstrong, Gene Krupa, and Harry James. At this time, Istanbul was often the first stop for American musicians going outside America. These were the impressions of America that were stamped in my memory bank.

I used to read in my father's restaurant—*Life Magazine,* the *Spiegel*, the *Paris Match*, and also four different Istanbul newspapers. On one occasion we saw my brother's picture— Peter Nova—in the paper *Hürriyet*. Along with his Turkish colleagues, he received his mechanical engineering degree from Purdue University in Indiana.

DREAMS WITHOUT SACRIFICE

I think the toughest thing in any cosmopolitan society is to have *Unity in Diversity,* creating an atmosphere where every culture is expected to respond to one set of values.

It is very difficult to sacrifice the idea that your religion or culture is the best and superior to all others.

There were many European Institutions established in Istanbul of the 1900s. such as the French High School (*Notre dame de Sion*) and the Saint George Hospital where the nun nurses worked tirelessly in their duties for doctors and surgeons.

Also, there were the Italian High School, the Greek, German, Armenian, Slav, Bulgarian, Russian, American and Jewish Organizations, each serving the needs of its respective ethnic group. But according to my older generation, these cultures would not sacrifice for unity, so they were unable to confront the coming crisis, which would result in the demise of Istanbul's multicultural society.

My father, after working very hard to establish himself in business, community and the Church, was one of the exceptions. He worked very hard to lead his fellows into unity and brotherhood. His Turkish philosophy was: *The summer does not come with one flower. We need many more flowers to keep the unity alive!*

I walked in his path, but it was too late to avoid the coming trouble.

THE CYPRUS CRISIS

Cyprus is a significant island in the northeast of the Mediterranean, 40 miles from the south of Turkey, and 60 miles from Syria and Palestine. About three-fourths of its population is Greek and one-fourth is of Turkish origin. Cyprus had been under the Ottoman Empire since 1570, and in 1878 the Ottomans sold it to Great Britain. In the 1950s when the Greek Cypriots started guerilla attacks for Independence, the troubled British politicians went back to Turkey and asked them to pursue their rights. Since the British were leaving Cyprus, they wanted *to retain control of their two bases along the southern part of the island which was close to Israel.*

This act ignited the forgotten hatred and conflict between Greece and Turkey (which had been curtailed by Atatürk and

Venizelos in the 1930s). These two leaders of rival countries had had great understanding for each other's country and they kept the peace, but now they were gone.

One of the reasons for the September 6-7 Tragedy in 1955 was a mistake on the part of the Turkish Government. They allowed big demonstrations in Istanbul against the Greek Government and the supporters of the Megalo Idea, which in Greek means, *Big Idea*. Without realizing that a big crowd of organized mobs were demolishing any Greek-related business, churches and the wealth of the minorities, the government allowed the situation to worsen. *Kin gözünü bürümüş* is a Turkish saying: *The hate has blinded the eyes!*

The crisis could have been prevented by America, but President Johnson was very busy with Vietnam, and the following years when the situation for Istanbul minority was worsening in 1969 to the point that was unbearable, President Nixon had left Secretary of the State Kissinger in full charge of the Middle East problems. As a result, Kissinger paid only "lip service" to the Istanbul minority and devoted his energies towards aiding Israel.

CRISIS AND RELIGION

By observing the consequences of the Cyprus crisis in 1955, I don't think the leaders of our religion helped the dream of my parents and other faithful Christian friends because they did not pay much attention to the relationship with Muslims and poor people in the countryside of Anatolia.

The Orthodox Greeks had twelve highly-paid bishops with private cars and chauffeurs in Istanbul, who were not allowed to marry, but they had their secret girlfriends.

As a kid we had to listen to their preaching and kiss their hands, and we had to listen to the fanatic followers telling us that the true Christians are the Orthodox Greeks. Like today's Pope's primacy message in Matthew 18:20, Jesus is among the two or three gathered in his name and they are the *Catholics* who are the *True Christians* (Fall of 2007).

I saw how being religiously judgmental could bring the demise of a Cosmopolitan culture, as in the case of the Greek Orthodox community in Istanbul, which prevailed in the 30s thru 50s.

According to my older Greek Orthodox friend Thanasi who had served three years the Turkish military, the Greek minority in Istanbul (called Rum by the Turks) had done bad things in the 30s and 40s, serving the Greek Idea and never saying, *I am first a Turkish citizen and then a member of my ethnic community.*

They never had the Turkish flag on one side and the Greek flag on the other side inside the church like we do in the U.S.A.

Also, he remembers the scam of the gold market during WWII, which was organized by three individuals of Istanbul—one Greek, one Armenian, and a Jew. They traveled around the countryside paying a lot of cash for the gold by lying to the farmers and people that the gold will lose its value. And after buying up enough gold, they were able to raise the price of gold in the market.

During this time the Prime minister was the victorious general, İsmet İnönü, who uncovered the causal factors of the gold scam, and apparently he had bad impressions of those greedy individuals and the minority.

It is common for people to remember the bad things of any age and forget the good ones.

Also, I was surprised during my military service in Anatolia 1956-58 to find out how poor the people were in contrast to the prosperous rich in Istanbul.

This was bothering my mind, I wanted to find out what the rich and established businessmen in Istanbul were thinking about, so in a conversation with a millionaire businessman I asked him what in his and others opinions would help the situation? He responded: "You, young man, don't worry about the poor, you just take care of your father's business and everything will be O.K.!" This mindset revealed that the culture of Istanbul was not established in the hearts of the Turkish people.

I began thinking logically about the phrase used in theology (like my father's Greek philosophy): *With the mind and the knowledge many people found God.* Many hold the theory—a theory held by those who reverence bigger church buildings, like Saint Sophia's Church, and Turkish Ayasofya (one of the Seven Architectural Wonders), in Istanbul—that you reach God by *size,* and when you do God will save you from any trouble. However, it should be obvious that this theory doesn't work in the real universe.

We need more understanding in the world community.

CHAPTER III: The Boot Camp

I was drafted in 1956 for two years to the Turkish military, just after the explosive incidents against Christians in Istanbul (Sept. 6-7, 1955) named by the *Greek Orthodox Observer* in 2005 as the "Pogrom of Constantinople."

I remember the day I had to be ready in the recruit center for the boot camp in Anatolia (Asia minor), one of the toughest boot camps in the world. The Turkish military wanted us to be Rambos, to be able to survive without water and food in the desert or jungle for days and use the bayonet and rifle very efficiently for self-defense. As I was bidding farewell to my family, my mother wouldn't stop crying, even when I tried to persuade her by saying, "This is not going to be risky because we don't have a war. It's just military training, duty, and return back to civil life."

So many of my cousins and friends were back from military training that I thought she shouldn't worry. We even knew of a Korean War veteran who had received a medal from Gen. McArthur. I found the reason she was crying was because of her memories of my father's experiences in WWII, when he was sent to a concentration camp. People said to her, "We don't know if he is going to come back!" But he returned, this time as a sergeant of the Christian Brigade in the Turkish military of Asia Minor, proving that he is a brave Albanian veteran (he served before in the Albanian military as an officer) to serve this time his new country. He is a reminder of the famous saying: *Tough times don't last, but tough people, they do last.*

Finally my mother ceased weeping and her consciousness returned. She told me the famous Albanian proverb: "What the Government does to you, God doesn't do to you. I raised you with faith and affection, so don't forget that God will help you overcome the tough times."

I was a hard worker, trained by my father in the slaughterhouse, and in the busy restaurant by my uncle Michael (my father's partner) who was the symbol of toughness.

A summer day at the island with my cousin Thomas

Also, I thought that being an athlete, a swimmer in 1500 meters (placed in the top 10 in Turkey in 1955) should have made it easy for me in the boot camp, but surprisingly I found that something tougher waiting for me. I was sent to a place with over 2000 youngsters from Anatolia who didn't know how to speak Turkish! Maybe the Government and Military wanted the young men from Istanbul with affluence to be deprived in Military service by sharing the pain of being poor? Not being able to talk or share thoughts with a comrade or human being for weeks —that was really torture.

During the brutal training boot camp, the brain quits functioning and grows numb. Not long before the end of the boot camp, a Captain with documents in his hand showed up and started talking to me in English. He said, "This paper says you know English. We can use your help. Is this right?"

I could not answer him in English or in Turkish, so my eyes were filled with tears, staring at him. He understood right away what was going on and he told me, "You are going to be O.K in a few days, so don't worry, I will take care of you. I have a strong message from your father to relieve you for a few days. The Army doesn't allow me to give you permission, but if you can disguise yourself, you can go to Istanbul. Don't get caught by the M.P." So, I was disguised as a farmer and I found a small airplane to fly me to Istanbul. The plane made me vomit, but I did not care, I was flying home!

At home, nobody recognized me. I was there also for my brother's wedding, who was marrying a Christian girl of Istanbul who was named Thomai. After the wedding, I met my accordion teacher Pandeli to tell him that I lost the ability to play the accordion. He comforted me saying that the ability would come back, to not worry, and in a few days he made me play again.

I returned to my post, and not long after, a general my father knew sent me to the 6th Division's Military Band to be part of the brass, and to also play accordion at the Military Casino for weddings and other events. I had a full schedule because I also had to learn the trumpet and train for the Marching Band and Concert Band, because we would be performing popular music for the high schools. I was also to help the officers train the illiterate soldiers to learn the musical notation. They had been playing instruments only by ear.

Military band of the sixth division

THE WILD BIRDS

One of my achievements as I made more friends in the band was when I saw three gypsy soldiers learning notation. They were having a tough time with the drill sergeant. They were beaten for not learning as quickly as he wanted. Because I listened to them at nights in the barracks playing their instruments beautifully in the gypsy Alaturka, music filled with pain and melancholy, I decided to ask permission from the Band Master to instruct them. What I did was to tell them to understand we have to finish our duty for the country. I said, "Look at me, I am from the city and you are from the countryside. You are playing your instruments as beautifully as the wild birds in the mountains, but God brought us together to help each other. I am your friend and I will help you learn notation the easy way. I will also help you learn the marches and other types of music you need to know."

In a few days the gypsies began learning fast. They became part of the band playing with skill their brand new instruments they had received from the General Marshall. (General Marshall is the man who predicted that after the World War II, America would need more allies to fight Communism for the free world). It was so amazing that those Gypsies were made a separate team when performing their Alaturka Music for weddings and other special events. The officers (Music Institute graduates) and I could not understand their ability to improvise in each performance a different Cadenza! We felt that they must be inspired from God, like the wild birds.

Playing the accordion in the military jazz band

I loved my silver cornet made in U.S.A, I enjoyed performing in the concert band for the holidays, yet I often met school children who could not afford having any instruments! I could have saved my cornet, but after twenty years, I didn't know that I had to buy a Japanese Yamaha trumpet for my son Eric in America for his High School marching band.

It was tough to play the cornet during winter's freezing weather, to raise the flag and other activities. Sometimes we had to run around the field by holding the instrument under the military coat to warm it up

**My veteran friend Ismail with his Sousaphone
and me with the cornet .**

HE CALLED ME BROTHER

My friend Ismail from Istanbul had a tough time with his Tuba, a Bb sousaphone (which is bigger than the Eb sousaphone). I did my best to help him not hate this wonderful instrument, which was so heavy and awkward it hurt his shoulder. (Thankfully, now there are lighter tubas for young musicians). I helped him practice "Stars and Stripes Forever" as well as the Turkish Marches. Ismail owned a bookstore in Istanbul that would delight any university professor, a place where one could find history books containing information spanning fifteen centuries!

We were required to play Chopin's "Funebra March" for the fallen F14 jet pilots from the airbase next to us) killed occasionally in war exercises and for other military events. On November 10 there is an annual Memorial Parade honoring Atatürk. I felt such great sorrow for the Turkish Nation losing such a great man, and I was motivated to write a Waltz Triste in his honor.

It was a real joy to play the songs of Johann Strauss, J. Philip Sousa and other composers at military events. In summer our jazz band played to entertain the colonels and generals in the Military Vacation Camp (Erdek).

These older officers had young Turkish wives who often flirted with us, which posed a real danger. In those times, a Christian flirting with a Muslim girl meant risking your life. Later when I was married, I found out that my wife's uncle, who was a prominent *maitre d'hotel* (manager of hotel) of Ankara Palace in the 1950s, had a Turkish mistress and was shot by her brother!

36

My late wife's uncle as a manager of the Ankara palace

In Istanbul we had a more open and accepting interracial society. For example, our neighbor, Turkish Navy Colonel Cemal, married a Greek girl, even though he had to resign as a Naval officer. And my close friend, the Turkish swim champion, Enver, (a Muslim) married a Jewish girl.

THE TURKISH OFFICER

I was lucky that I had studied accordion. The Master Sergeant (Turgut Çalışal) Instructor of the Band, was a virtuoso with his clarinet and he had an amazing perfect pitch, He was the head of our Jazz-Dance Band with his clarinet, as well as alto sax. He also loved the accordion, sometimes asking me to play a *pasadoble* or *valse musette* saying, " I have to clean the rust of my ear from the daily noises of the band and military buff." He was a very tough man, daring, often in conflict with the high officers and yet getting away with it, because he was highly respected by the General. He had also a medal from Gen. McArthur in Korea.

Here comes the story of the Turkish officer which proves the Turkish proverb:

"There Are No Bad People, Only Bad Individuals"

After a while the soldier musicians of the band realized that I was not Muslim. They were confused and they were telling me: *You are so good. You have to be a Muslim. How come you are Christian?* I tried to explain my beliefs that there were many religions in the world and suggested that we talk about that subject later. I realized that every human being believes his religion is the best.

It was interesting that I had a conversation with a soldier who was a clerk with a Turkish name, and he observed my interaction with the fellow Muslim soldiers.

He saluted me one day and said, "Anesti, you are doing a good job in the band, but you could have also piece of mind if you have changed your name to a Turkish name like I did! I was surprised to find out that he was a Jew.

"Sorry," I said to him. My father's guiding proverb has always been: *Never try to hide your identity and be brave to live with that.* The Turks say *Aslını inkar eden evgittir,* which in English means, *Whoever denies his identity is gypsy.* But on the basis of my experience, I disagree with the derogatory comments about gypsies.

The Master Sergeant must have noticed some tension because he asked me if those soldiers were putting pressure on me to change my religion. I said, "No, they are good kids, they are just wondering, expressing their thoughts." He was not satisfied with my explanation; he wanted to teach them a lesson. One early morning he assembled the band and said: "I have an order from the Government to make you all Christians!" A loud sound came from the crowd protesting the sergeant, they thought he was crazy.

He said, "What? You didn't like it? Why then do you want Anesti to be a Muslim? He came with his faith to finish his military service, and don't forget, we believe in the same God he believes in! *Bir Allah*, (which in Turkish means, "God is one.") So go back to your duty and leave him alone to help us better for our destination to accomplish our goal of building a better civilization. Atatürk said: 'Our biggest enemy is illiteracy.' I was surprised to hear this from a Turkish Muslim officer!

I wonder how many leaders realize the truth of Atatuürk's theory. It is interesting and amazing that in America we have people who are very narrow minded, and I believe their mindset places them on a similar level as illiterate people.

I have suggested since I came to U.S.A that we should legislate a draft of one or two years for young people to serve their country in a different area from where they live.

This would give them an opportunity of better understanding each other.

CHAPTER IV: Music Education in Germany and the *Parole d'honneur*

After my military service ended, I returned to help my father in the restaurant and establish myself as a new manager. Because my father knew my desire for classical music, he sent me after a year in 1959 to Germany to Trossingen Stadt. Musikschule, the top school for classical accordion.

Here the school gave me a full scholarship and a pass for free lunch. The only problem was that the lessons were taught in German. Because I loved to study there, I put pressure on myself to learn German (my sixth language). In two months I was able to understand the teachers in the class. That was a record for foreign students; so the Director Dr. Armin Fett gave me the title (Polyglot) Multilingual. I worked very hard to take the best classes in piano, performance, *Contrapunkta,* and composition. I also enjoyed the experience of being a member in the choir of Beethoven's Ninth. This was possible because the town of Trossingen was preparing for a grand opening of the new Concert Hall with a production of Beethoven's Ninth, which required almost 100 people to sing in the choir.

Conductor Walter Hugler, who was also professor in our school for Music-History, and who was conducting and analyzing Beethoven's work, recruited and organized male and female singers to sing with the Stuttgart Philarmonia. It was amazing to see our professor conductor conduct the orchestra, cueing us in the entries of different passages in German.

I also met the twentieth century composer, Prof. Paul Hindemith, when he came to conduct a concert in Trossingen and visit our school.

I enjoyed studying with international students— Americans, Danish, Norwegian, Finish, Yugoslavian, and Hungarian—and I made an effort to learn their languages and cultures and to listen to their touching stories. For example, two Hungarian friends explained to me how they walked two days and nights through the woods to escape the Russian tanks in Budapest and reach Austria and then moved on to Germany. One student from East Germany was able to jump over the Berlin wall and enter the school to become an accordion teacher. He taught me some Russian. It was nice to learn the accordion *bellow shake technique* from my Norwegian friend Marlow Sorrenson (a student of the famous Toralf Tollafsen) and become the first accordionist to perform this technique with one of the heaviest accordions in the world. The German friends used to call me, *Die verrückte Akkordion spieler*, which in German means, *the crazy accordionist*. In my study of languages, I discovered that the Hungarian and Finish have the same alphabet. Consequently, I acquired the reputation as the man with his copybook.

During my music education, a coup occurred in Turkey. The government led by the popular Prime Minister, Adnan Menderes, was overthrown in this military coup. My father was not able to send me my monthly allowance because the banks were not transferring money to Europe. Therefore, I had to find a job; I was fortunate to find one in the Hohner accordion factory next to the school.

During my job I made some friends, one in particular was a German friend who was an anti-Nazi during the war. He told me that there were some young ex-S.S. officers working in the factory. I was curious to meet them even though my friend said they wouldn't talk to me. I approached one of them with a political trick in my head. I introduced myself as a Turkish student from Turkey, the only country that did not fight Germany in WWII and one that was an ally in WWI. After a few efforts he started expressing his feelings that Germany had to rise again from this misery and occupation and once again resurrect the third Reich! When I was in Stuttgart, I gave this information to British-Americans and they thanked me.

During my second year in Musik Schule Trossingen, I received a letter from my parents with their picture requesting that I return to Istanbul, because my father was ill. Seeing the picture of my father made me realize that they were serious.

Because of these circumstances, I went to Dr. Armin Fett (Director of the school) and explained to him that my father was ill and the honorable thing was for me to return home to take over the family business as I had promised before I went to Germany.

He was surprised to learn that I was leaving, because he wanted me to stay longer in the school for the Solisten Class including instructions, and to send me anywhere in the Western hemisphere as an Harmonika-accordion instructor, because of the languages I knew already and the additional languages I was learning from other international students.

During this time, the production of the special accordions made by Hohner was flourishing in sales. They had invented the Baritone basses, and elevated these instruments to a classical level, with cooperation of Italian masters like Morino and Gola.

I was honored by my director's vision for my future. However, "the dye was cast" and my decision was to stay with my *parole d'honneur,* which in English means, *Word of honor to my father.*

MEETING THE RUSSIANS

Before returning to Istanbul, I traveled to Italy with my Italian friend, Nino, and stayed in his sister's house in Verona. I then went to Lido, Venice, in Trieste I decided to take a Russian passenger ship to Istanbul with the idea of meeting Russians.

Two American professors were also in the ship and to them I demonstrated the accordion with the Russian song "Minka." The Russians listening were impressed. Then I met a Russian doctor who played the piano. I played Liszt and he played Rachmaninoff, who said that music always connects us and sometimes helps us to feel free again.

In Istanbul, trouble was waiting for me. The Turkish version of the F.B.I. held me for interrogation as a possible spy. After an hour, I was able to prove to the chief that I was a musician and very interested in other people's music, and not politics.

In 1962 I had a concert in Istanbul with my colleague and the top German accordion virtuoso, Jürgen Löchter, introducing for the first time the classical accordion and the bellow shake technique. The dream of having of a concert tour in the Balkans felt apart because of the deterioration of the status of minorities in Istanbul. Also, because of my father's health, I had to concentrate on the restaurant business.

THE MATCHMAKER

Through the efforts of my matchmaker mother—whose title in the Greek Albanian community was "The Lady with the Red Bag"—the following year I married a girl, Ilektra, after a one-year engagement. My mother knew many families, and she used to name the nice and sensible girls *Kalogre,* which in Albanian means, *Nun.*

After a careful search, she found a pearl in a poor section of Istanbul for me! The young girl's parents and brother lived in an apartment building built by the World Council of Churches, which was known as *Dostluk evi* in Turkish.

My mother anticipated that the gossips would wag their tongues to belittle this girl from a poor family. They would use the old Albanian expression and say that she was "taking her shoes off to enter the wealth" and was only looking for expensive finery. My wise mother had no tolerance for gossip and jealousy and for such wags she prepared a special comeback: *God gave us wealth and we will provide whatever she desires.*

This was modern matchmaking. Young people were introduced to each other and in our case, my parents invited the girl with her parents and brother to a *casino* for a dinner. (A casino in Istanbul was a place for dining and dancing and watching a live show, but not for gambling as in America)

This first meeting gave the couple a chance to see if they were interested each other. In my case, I told the parents that I would not decide now, but I will like to meet her alone and to share with her my ideas and what were my expectations of a wife.

We were engaged for a year, and we agreed to take care of my parents (even that was considered old fashioned) and we moved to a modern apartment with seven rooms to live together. Unfortunately, my older sister had just divorced in Germany and came back to live with us.

After 1964 the situation of minorities became worse because of the Cyprian crisis. We were treated as if we guilty of supporting the Greeks' wanting annex Cyprus! The Greek prime minister did not want to share the island with its 30% Turkish population. We knew the Greek did not give a damn for the minorities in Istanbul.

THE OLD WOLF

At that time the Prime Minister of Turkey was İsmet İnönü, the victorious general of the 20's for Liberation. He had served with Atatürk. The Greeks did not perceive him to be an "old wolf" in negotiations, so they were caught by surprise when he gave orders to expel the Greek citizen Greeks in Istanbul, where they had been allowed to stay and prosper since 1928, according to the Lausanne Treaty which was signed in Europe by İsmet İnönü himself!

I was surprised when a friend, Iraklis Bekos, who had studied with me at the same Greek private school I attended, told me that he had to leave the country in 48 hours. When I asked my father what the heck was going on, he told me. He said that those Greek citizens should have applied for Turkish citizenship long ago like my father did, even if it meant they had to experience the hardship of being drafted into the military for a short time.

He quoted a Greek proverb: "Sins of the parents tortures the kids."

There was no exception to this expulsion order, even for my first accordion teacher Pandeli Citra, who had been congratulated by the master sergeant of the military band in the

45

name of the Turkish military because he had sent good musical students to serve the country.

It was too late to stop his deportation when I found out. With the help of my father and his connections, I could have at least helped my teacher.

A MOTHER'S LEGACY

The year of 1966 began with happiness but ended with great sadness. My mother had the urge to see my older brother, and I was able to send my parents to the U.S.A to visit him, his wife and two daughters. Upon their return, my mother was very happy that she was able to spend time with her first living son and his family, and to see America. She was very complimentary and gave me all the blessings she had in Albanian: *God give you health and good kids that they will give you happiness you deserve*, etc. In the meantime, my wife was expecting and all of us were happy. Suddenly my mother had a serious stroke (having survived a previous one). Unfortunately, she passed away at the age of 62 with an unfinished job of caring for my father who was fighting his own battle with *arteriosklerosis.*

In the funeral mass, there were many people both in and outside the church. After the burial, many strangers gave me condolences. Because I did not recognize them, I asked who they were. It turned out that they were individuals my mother had secretly helped them through the years. It was then that I remember her leaving the house without telling us where she was going. That brought me peace and healing to my grief.

MY SON'S BAPTISM AND
A CHANGING CHURCH

After three months my wife gave birth to my son Eric, his name actually was İraklis, Greek: Hercules. In 1967 when I looked into having him baptized, I found that the Greek Orthodox Church had developed degrees of service—first class, second class, third class—for baptisms, weddings, burials, etc., according to an arbitrary class system and one's social standing. I was disgusted to learn that in third class some of the lights were shut down in the church ceremony. I complained to the Patriarch that according to Jesus teachings, there should be a full service of the church for rich or for poor!

I made my point. Since then, as far as I know, there have been no degrees of services for the Greek Orthodox Church in Istanbul.

CHAPTER V: Walking on the Embers of the Old Hate

During difficult times as a Christian of the Greek Orthodox Church in Istanbul, I did my best to follow the steps of my father who was highly respected as a sergeant during WWII. He became Benefactor Trustee of the Greek Orthodox Church, and along with retired Albanian General Cemal Aranitas, co-founded the Turkish-Albanian Association

Because of my father's deteriorating health, I operated my father's busy restaurant without losing my concentration as a boss of ten Turkish Muslim employees by *walking on the embers of the old hate.*

I was fortunate to have mastered the skill of understanding and treating people as equals. I studied the Kurdish language so as to deal effectively with my subordinates—topnotch hard workers but illiterate. Eventually I taught them Turkish. In turn they gave me the nickname, *Apo*, meaning uncle in Kurdish, which was their way of saying, I was one of them.

It should be noted that the Kurdish minority had jobs in Istanbul and lived peacefully under the rules of Atatürk who said: *I am a Turk and you will be treated as an equal.* In Turkish, this would be said, *Ne mutlu Türküm diyene.*

Unfortunately Atatürk did not live long enough to prevent the growth of population from 18 million to 70 million and the penetration of the fanatical Muslims. This resulted in the obstruction of reforms established by him. One major reform was the separation of the state from religion, the first time in history for this to be accomplished in a Muslim Country!

THE DEATH OF A CUSTOMER IN THE RESTAURANT

One day an incident occurred in our restaurant. A customer died of a fatal heart attack while eating a bowl of tripe soup. I remember seeing the other customers who were at his table jumping up in fright, calling to me upon seeing this man's head face down in his bowl of soup.

Everyone was in shock, and I knew I had to act right away. I first closed the restaurant, and then, called the police, who sent a coroner, who in old Turkish was known as *Mudeiumumi.*

My manager, Dursun Çavus, knowing this customer was Muslim, ran to the nearest mosque, Tophane Cami, to inform the Imam, the spiritual leader. A simple casket was brought to the restaurant and the deceased was placed in it, and with help of the other employees, the body was taken to the mosque.

As a Christian I had to refrain from helping in order to avoid any blame from his relatives. It was different in the military service when a soldier in our company died. Then, I attended the Muslim service and prayed with and performed the ritual act—*Namaz kılma.*

In spite of the care I had taken on the day of the Muslim's death, the next day the son of the deceased visited me. I knew him as an unhappy man with a strong bias about wealthy Christians, and he considered me very lucky to be owner of this restaurant.

He said, "I can go after you for indemnity because my father died in your restaurant, but I see you have a very strong group of Muslim workers who defend you strongly."

It was true that my workers had a great respect for my father and me. I followed the established rules of the

49

organization created by my father and consequently he had no reason to allege misconduct under my leadership.

There was another incident when a worker came to my defense. He was one of the younger cooks named, Tandırcı Halil. On seeing an undercover cop from the Turkish F.B.I. (*Tarı memuru* in Turkish) giving me a hard time, he confronted him by saying, "Our boss is a very knowledgeable man and he can speak more languages than our Prime Minister, so you better treat him nice."

FACING THE FEAR AND DECISION TO COME TO AMERICA

One of my life's formidable tests occurred on a day when a large mob planed public demonstrations against the Government of Cyprus (1969).

The news came rapidly and minority businesses closed their stores to leave the Main street barren except for my open restaurant.

My senior cook advised me to leave and go home. He said, "It is not a good time to be around and we want you to be safe." I said, "I don't think so. What will happen will happen (*Que sera sera*)." I had to show that as a descendent of my father's heritage (Brave Epirus, in southern Albania), I was not afraid.

This pending crisis aroused me to recall there are two kinds of bravery: One in military and another in civil life. The latter enabled me to stand strong against Muslim demonstrators intending to destroy my restaurant. Meanwhile, the neighboring stores received telephone calls to find out where I was and why I was not at home.

When the crowd of demonstrators drew near to the restaurant, I was standing in front of the door with all my employees by my side.

The front line of the marching crowd stopped for an instant when they saw me standing there defying the danger. They were confused, so they started marching again, yelling slogans, throwing articles to break the windows of the restaurant...I survived this attack, but another one was in the waiting.

Another day walking down the street to take the Ferryboat to the Island a demonstrator who was an anarchist tried once again to kill me with his knife which resulted in a leg wound while I was defending myself.

It was nice to see the Muslim business people rushing to my help and calling the police. I had a tough time hiding my bloody clothes from my wife, who was already very worried.

But the confidence of my workers and neighbors was great, and I gained strength to concentrate in my work.

I tried my best, but the situation worsened, and the leaders of two countries were not negotiating. They continued to argue over the ownership of Cyprus and like the Turkish expression, *Karpuz başıma patlıyor*, the watermelon was smashing down on my head.

No matter how brave and righteous you are, the flood of hate can cover and drown everything.

In 1970 my father died after suffering four years from Arteriosklerosis without seeing and realizing the demise of his dream for Istanbul. He often said, "The Cosmopolitan life in Istanbul will stay."

The principal of the Greek school where Eric (my son) was in kindergarten told me that next year they can't enroll him because he is Albanian Orthodox and not Greek Orthodox (a new law from the Government of İsmet İnönü).

That was the straw that broke the back of the camel. So I decided that it was time to leave, even at the cost of losing the wealth that my father had accumulated. I would not accept the law stopping me from sending my son to the school I wanted him to attend! I didn't want to raise my son in a mess where he could suffer later.

I had made the decision to leave Istanbul. My first thought was that maybe I should think of moving to Athens, because I had friends and relatives (including my sisters) in Greece.

But, my memories of my early contact with the American Navy changed my mind. The spirit of 1776 suddenly overpowered my thoughts: "We the people, for the people, to serve the interest of all people-rich and poor, to guarantee to everyone the freedom of speech, religion and of the press." With these things in my mind, I saw a better future for my son and family in America.

There was also a possibility of imminent war and the Turks would likely call back veterans to send them to the front. I was blessed to come to America on time in 1972 with my brother's affidavit support, gained because of his position as an executive in America. Some Christian friends in Cyprus were not as lucky because they died when Turkish combat forces invaded.

CHAPTER VI: Coming to America in 1972

My wife, my son Eric (five years old) and I were in the Atatürk airport of Istanbul ready to take the plane to America. My folks were there to wish us good luck and good-bye. While we waited on our flight, the Airport authority called our names and asked us to report to the desk. We did as the intercom announcement had directed and were told that we couldn't leave that day.

I asked the Inspector what the reason for the delay. I said I should have the freedom to travel anywhere since I had served this country for two years in Military and had represented Turkey in Germany in classical music!

He apologized and said that it was not in his hands, that the Government from Ankara ordered that Christians weren't allowed leave the country till the government checked to see if they owed tax money.

I could not understand how the hell I had ended up in a such a weird situation in Istanbul. Personally, I was dumfounded. My family and I were model citizens and hard workers who paid every bill and tax, having faith, serving the country, always respecting helping other people, and then to leave like guilty person. During the past years many Christian business people who owed millions in tax money had left the country with no trace, and I who had always paid my taxes could not!

The Greek proverb says : Πλαi στο ξερο καiγετε και το χλορο, which means, *In the fire, next to the dry one burns also the wet one.* This is not fair. How are politicians and governments able to destroy the life of a society so easily?

MARKO PASHA

The tragicomedy was that we did not have "Marko Pasha" to complain to him. In an old Istanbul joke, it was said that in old times, Marko Paşa was a Christian general assigned by the Sultan as the Ministry to handle the complaints!

Even in Turkish we say: *Güvendiğin dağlara kar yağdı,* which means, *The mountains you were depending on are covered with heavy snow and you can't reach them!*

I had to listen to my poor wife, who was poor indeed before she married me, and had been a wealthy housewife enjoying Istanbul for eight years. She now condemned the people who caused the demise of her Cinderella life.

If I have to talk realistically in the name of the Christian minority in Istanbul of the 40's and 50's, we never called ourselves first Turkish citizen and then our ethnic group. The same is true in America where we have too many citizens who don't say: I am first American and then I am _____ (their ethnicity).

This mentality was the seed of a perpetual hate and we were not aware of the catastrophe it would create in the long run to the Cosmopolitan culture of Istanbul, an environment created by Atatürk, who was 80 years ahead of his time. One of his teachings was: *The greatest enemy of a civilization is illiteracy in history and not learning or understanding the other cultures!*

I was angry in the airport over the delay, but my accountant and friend Apostol comforted me by promising to solve the problem.

The second day we were again in the airport after my accountant worked hard with the tax department and various officials. But every announcement in the speakers was a nightmarish anguish, fear that our names would be called again saying that we can't go, that we have to pay for the sins of other's. We even had a fear that even when the plane took off, they might call the plane back!

Finally, we found ourselves in Kennedy airport in New York. It was in New York that I expected to get a job with Hohner's exports center. When I looked into renting an apartment, and saw all the high-rise apartments with the fire escapes behind them, I couldn't envision my son and wife who spoke no English living there. I had saved them from a war, and felt it didn't make sense to have them live in the jungle of New York.

I have wondered if I did not have such negative thoughts about living conditions in New York, I may have been able to get a job as interpreter in the United Nations since I had a solid knowledge of six languages and a smattering of a couple more.

THE FORK IN THE ROAD

But I took another avenue in the fork in the road of life seeking more stability in my new country. We went to Bridgeport, Connecticut to stay with my cousin who had immigrated to the U.S. fifteen years before. He owned a small grocery store which he managed with his wife and son. In 1972 he was not aware that Bridgeport had many war industry jobs because of the Vietnam War, but it had become a dead city for jobs after the end of the war! After two months of looking for a job, finally I took a job in a small factory. The company was Porter Box, where I worked as a power saw operator for two dollars and a quarter per hour! The old and unsafe power tools in the shop were causing accidents to the workers. One accident happened to me with the power saw and I lost a part of my left hand finger, which could have ended my performing on accordion. After surgery I was fortunate not to lose the joint of

55

the finger and it healed in a way that it did not interfere with my playing

As an accordion teacher with a degree from Germany, I could not find any students, because everybody wanted to learn guitar for rock and roll music. Nobody wanted to learn the accordion.

Even in Thomaston, which is a German town, the kids won't spend the energy required to master their traditional instrument. The kingdom of the accordion was over. I even had an interview in Bridgeport University demonstrating my classical accordion for music teachers, who were impressed, but they told me that if I wanted to obtain a job as a public school teacher, I had to go back to college with two years credit because of my degree in music. I knew it would be impossible to attend college with a wife and a kid who needed financial support.

One music teacher discouraged me from devoting the time required to become a public teacher because of low teacher salaries at that time (1972), but in the long run he proved to be wrong.

Needless to say, the times were very difficult and they had a painful effect of my wife. She watched me struggling to achieve the American Dream. She often told me the Greek saying : Απο Δημαρχος κλητηρας, which means in Greek: *After being a Mayor, to become an usher*!

OUR FIRST AMERICAN FRIENDS

We realized that living with relatives was not something we wanted as a permanent living situation. I found an apartment in a mid-upscale neighborhood in Trumbull, CT. Fortunately, we located next door to a newlywed couple who took us under their wing. Jim and Sally became our first American friends.

Jim would spend a lot of time with Eric after coming from his job, and Sally, who was a teacher, became friends with Ilektra. She also was teaching Eric English. In three months he was ready for the first grade. It was funny when Ilektra and Sally would go shopping because they would have to use Eric as a translator. After two hours Eric would tell them, "Time off! I can't do anymore."

Meanwhile, I was taking a course for Hotel-Motel management. After six months I found out that the only available jobs were in Western states. It was typical in a New York Hotel interview for job they asked me if I had experience of getting unpaid bills from the customers—that was too much for me.

We had a visit from my wife's cousin Arthur and his relatives Lee and George, who were from Hartford, CT. They spent some time trying to persuade us to move to Hartford, where there were more families from Istanbul.

I felt that this move would be good for Ilektra who wanted more old-country friends. In the meantime, I found a better job in Hartford after being one and half years in Bridgeport. We moved to East Hartford into the Deerfield apartments where the manager and future owner was Kelly Totonis from Istanbul. I also worked for him part-time as a painter.

MEMORIES OF A KID

I sent my wife and my son Eric, to Istanbul to her parents because she was homesick and lonely. It was interesting what a six-year-old kid can remember about his birthplace.

While they were in Istanbul, Eric asked his mother to go to the island, "Heybeliada," where we had a summerhouse. Because his mother did not want to see the house and feel bad, she made the mistake of lying, telling Eric that the house had burned up.

My son said, "It doesn't matter. I still want to go and see the stones and the place where I used to play and ride the donkey up and down the street." This made it more difficult for his mother who found that you can never lie to a kid who can put you in a more difficult position.

I don't know what she did after that, but when she turned back, in a party she shared her experience to people from Istanbul, which brought tears to their eyes.

After settling down in our new environment of Hartford, I applied for a job in Hartt School of Music, but there were no jobs for a music teacher in New England whose major instrument was the accordion. If I had known the rules of the school, I could have said that my major instrument is the trumpet and piano! In other states outside New England the accordion was accepted as a major instrument, but I didn't want to move again.

CHAPTER VII: Life in Restaurant Work

After losing hope of making a living by teaching accordion, I started working for restaurants. At that time Kentucky Fried Chicken had openings for manager trainees, and they offered a good salary and benefits.

I applied and started training for the franchise. Between 30-40 applicants started the training but only three and myself qualified to finish the three-month training course to become an assistant manager.

At that time it was difficult to become a cook for the franchise, because the chickens had to be prepared in pressure cookers, as Colonel Sanders directed by and only skilled workers were considered for this dangerous job. The floors were greasy and on the wall was a sign saying, "Think Chicken," which made me think this was an American "style" of motivating the workers to concentrate more.

I used to help some college graduates who were manager trainees like me to work safely on the greasy floor and steadied them as much as I could before they broke their neck on the concrete floor or metal tables. It made me realize the value of my old experience in the slaughterhouse, trained by my father to walk through the bloody mess across the slick floors.

The company competed with McDonalds and others for fast food service, so a lot of precooked chicken was thrown out at the end of the day. I started as an assistant manager with my experience of the old country and projected that I could reduce the waste, from 15% to 1 or 2% percent. When I succeeded, one of the executives from the headquarters visited me to find out how I was doing this.

He must have told the managers to follow my steps and reduce the waste; consequently, they began to label me a troublemaker to their (easy style) and started to discredit my theories to the director with negative reports.

A female cashier who did not like how the managers treated me gave me this information.

During this time my wife, Ilektra, wanted another child so Eric my firstborn son would have a sibling. She had a motherly feeling for her son, not to be alone in a foreign country. As the pregnancy progressed, the doctor who would give the prenatal care and deliver the baby, told me to contact the hospital.

When I went to the hospital, I found that I was not covered by my work insurance. I called the company to ask them why they did not enroll me with insurance since they had promised me this benefit as part of my employment.

The director of the company said, "We are going to put you on now." I said it was too late; the insurance for maternity had to be in effect six or nine months before delivery. I was really angry and wanted to sue them for lying or for exploiting a hard-working family man.

DAVID AGAINST GOLIATH

I went to the association's lawyer to get help. The lawyer told me that it was not Kentucky Fried Chicken, but the giant "Heublein" who owns K.F.C. and they have ten lawyers whose job was to stop any legal action against Heublein. I told him, "Look, I don't care how big they are. I worked very hard for them and I want them to pay for this.

The lawyer believed in me and did his homework. Before he went to the court he called the secretary of K.F.C. pretending that he was a businessman who wanted to review my working records before hiring me. The records indicated I was one of the top hard workers who finished the training and had become assistant manager with no absenteeism.

When we went to the court it was interesting to see the lawyers finding excuses to defend their company by stating that I was new in the country with not enough English to negotiate and manage their work, etc. The judge interrupted them by asking them how long their training program was and how long I had been working for them. After considering the information, the judge said, "This family man has been working for you for one and a half years. You have done wrong and you must pay him." This was a relief and great comfort for me to find out that there were good judges and justice in my new country.

Later on I had another restaurant managerial job in downtown Hartford, where the owners wanted me to fire and hire work personnel on a regular basis. I did not agree with their direction and quit again for another job that dealt with chemicals. The organization was called Swift and Sons.

In 1974 I became a father once again to my second son Jim, and my older son Eric was very happy to have a baby brother.

SMALL BUSINESS

Three years later came an opportunity to start my own pizza restaurant in Tolland next to Cumberland Farms as "Kent Pizza."

This location was the fourth Kent pizza developed by a Greek man who was a good pizza maker and he had in his mind the desire to make money by building a franchise and selling them. I bought this place at a decent price but he did not tell me that the previous buyer was not a good businessman and he failed to build up the business.

It took six months to start building the business again because people in Tolland didn't know that a new management had taken over.

Because my wife had learned to make Turkish dishes and desserts as well as French pastry from her mother, my mother, and from her father (who was pastry chef in Hilton Hotel of Istanbul), I strongly suggested to her that it is time to get out of the house and get involved in the restaurant.

She had to learn fast in order to get the driver's license which would enable her to run errands, drive the boys to their school activities and come to the restaurant.

We had difficulty finding a good babysitter for Jim, but we had our good neighbors Mr. George and Mrs. Carmenalita (Italian descent) who took care of our sons for a few years till Eric became a teenager and Jim, an elementary school student.

Our salvation was the day care center, World of Children, which opened in Tolland, within ½ mile from the restaurant. My wife would take Jim to the day care and come to the restaurant to assist the lunch business.

Eventually Eric started helping me by learning the Pizza business and he became a skilled Pizza maker, shaping (opening) the dough in to the pans, and assisting us during the busy weekends.

My older son Eric in the marching band

In spite of spending time in the shop, he was able to maintain good grades in high school, playing the trumpet in the marching band. He also became a swimmer, trained by the Laurence Swim Club under the tough challenging swim coach Herb Haas, and he became the M.V.P. of the East Hartford High swim team. When he graduated, he made State in two sports: swimming and tennis.

We improved the Pizza dough and sauce with the best Mozzarella cheese and other ingredients. It was interesting to find out from some customers that their children would identify Kent Pizza as the very best and when their parents would buy pizza somewhere else, their children would complain, "This is not Kent Pizza!"

The teenagers not only liked our Pizza but also the prices. We introduced to Tolland the new Greek salad, as well as the best meatballs, sausages, roast beef baked and served with tomato sauce, simmered all day with special ingredients and spices. Also, we started baking Spinach Pie (Börek style) never seen before in Pizzerias, prepared by my mother-in-law and wife. The Baklava, Kadayıf (shredded wheat) which were the top desserts and the recipes were passed on to my wife from her father (Pastry Chef).

Unfortunately, my father-in-law, the Pastry Chef, passed away shortly after coming to America with his wife. So the French Patisserie did not become part of the dessert menu.'

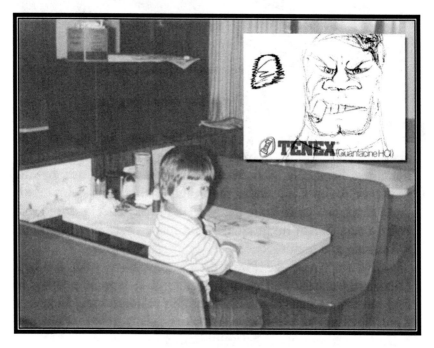

My younger son Jim became an artist in the restaurant drawing faces.

TACKY ITALIAN

Unknown to me, three staff members of *Interstate Gourmet Magazine* came to our restaurant and requested the specialties of the house.

As they left they said, "You are going to be in our magazine." When the article appeared, it praised our menu and the specialties, which included the Spinach Pie, Baklava, Kadayıf and stated that is not a "tacky Italian restaurant." This brought on the ire of the other Pizzerias in the area.

When a lady pizzeria owner called me and scolded me for my crude remarks about Italians, I replied, "If you have a complaint, you have to call the magazine because they wrote that comment. I don't even know what "tacky Italian" means."

Operating in Kent pizza restaurant

During this time we wanted to own our own home. I was trying to buy a nice condo unit in South Windsor where it was tough to get the best one.

We became friendly with the sister of the builder, Ms. Rose, who was the realtor of the Pleasant Hill condos, and when Ilektra baked her a spinach pie, that made the difference. She called me one day to tell me to come right away to put a deposit for a corner unit before somebody else gets it.

It was a townhouse unit with two floors and an unfinished basement. I had to transform the basement to a nice room for the Grandma, because I had the feeling she had the *idée fixe* (obsession) that basements are too damp and musty to live in.

As I predicted, when I showed her the unit and where she was going to sleep she said, "You are not going to throw me to the basement!" I was spending some effort to persuade her that it is not so, and the room will be nice for her when my sons defended me by informing her of the time and energy I had spent to transform this place into to a nice family room with a TV. Finally, she realized what a nice room she had, and equally important, she also enjoyed the company of her grandsons who spent ample time with her.

It came as a pleasant surprise to find what a big difference there existed in the educational system between East Hartford and South Windsor. Jim started a better education in the middle school, where the music program was terrific for his trombone playing and his mother attended all his school performances.

Performing Handel as a Trio Nova

LESSONS FROM AN EMPIRE AND THE PREDICTION

In the restaurant, I also started building personal relationships with the customers, who were interested in history, world events, and U.S foreign policy in the Middle East. Because, like my father, I was interested in history, reading many accounts about the great Empires, and Ottoman Empire, as well as the American history, which we called "Baby History" because it covered two centuries, I predicted, when America started believing in "Saddam Hussein", that he would fight for America against Iran. I also remember telling customers that this policy of giving so much military aid to Iraq would backfire in the long run. They thought I was not logical. Years later, when the customers remembered my prediction, they came to ask me, why didn't you tell our president? I said, "The White House never listens to an immigrant or other sources."

The Mutawakkilite Kingdom of Yemen (1918-1923) had a solid red flag. These days, politicians and the media are talking of connecting the dots, and are looking at the red flag of Yemen to do so. Tragically, the red flag was raised over 100 years before in the Yemen (under Ottoman Empire) that now dominates the nightly news. However, America has failed to look through the history window and, as a result, they are not able to read and understand the famous Turkish poem, "Adı Yemendir, giden gelmiyor, acep nedendir?" In English, this can be translated as a cry of the mothers of the land and means, The name is Yemen, whoever goes there doesn't come back. Why this is happening? The same red flag that was raised over 100 years before, and caused poets and mothers to question why an empire was losing their young sons in Yemen, has been raised again in America. And the mothers are still crying... I had even an interesting conversation with a British history professor who was visiting UConn. about the great movie "Laurence of Arabia."

My question was: Did Great Britain achieve a lot of things in the long run, or would it be better to leave them under the iron Turkish rule? The professor was taken back with my question. After a moment, he replied, "We have to admit that we did not achieve a lot. We caused also more pain than gain."

CHAPTER VIII: The Axe

When running your own business, it is very difficult to find time for family vacations. The only good time for vacation was to close down the first two weeks of August when "Pratt and Whitney" closed. And consequently many of our customers (P. &W. Engineers) went elsewhere to enjoy the days of a summer recess. It had been ten years since we opened the Pizza restaurant, and our lives were filled with restaurant work.

Our 25th Silver Anniversary was coming in 1988 and I decided in August to send my wife and two boys for a three week vacation to Athens, Greece to visit my two sisters. I would join them the last week of the vacation and then we would celebrate our anniversary.

It was a memorable anniversary with all our relatives and friends from Istanbul, and we enjoyed our much-needed vacation before returning to America fresh and ready to face the restaurant work.

The restaurant business was doing well and improving when Cumberland Farms (the owner of the plaza) decided to sell the plaza and left me with the option to either buy the plaza or get out. After discussing with my brother this business dilemma of purchasing the plaza at a fair price, the father of the company died and the sons took over. They had a different attitude about the business.

Instead of asking for a logical selling price from an immigrant of their faith—Greek Orthodox—and a man who suffered in Istanbul, who lost everything and then who worked for twelve years entirely devoted to making the restaurant a success, they closed the dairy store and gas station. Now, my business was the only one that continued to operate.

I took it upon myself to be the official caretaker, even spending time and money to take care of the well and pipes in the harsh winter months.

Five years later I lost the chance of having the total plaza because Cumberland Farms lost their property to a questionable "Eminent Domain" issue. It was like other great companies built by a father with ethics and then dismissed by their kids in America.

The year of 1989 is when our world fell apart. As human beings, young or old, we must deal with what comes on the road of life.

All the family was working hard, even Grandma who had to start the dough of the Spinach Pie, helping my wife to make it ready for the restaurant. Eric was already at the University of Connecticut majoring in engineering, and Jim was a student of South Windsor High school.

For some time my wife Ilektra had not felt well. Her doctor, a Russian immigrant, did not consider her symptoms very serious. Later on I was informed by our new doctor that women who finish menopause may be in a bigger danger of heart attacks than men, if they have genetically induced heart problems and high blood pressure.

One night after we went to bed my wife awoke early in the morning with chest pains. I said to her," I am taking you to the emergency this doesn't look good."

"No," she replied. "I am going to take some aspirin and I will be ok. I will go to see my doctor tomorrow."

There was no tomorrow for her, even though she went back to sleep and stayed in bed during the morning hours. Before I left for the restaurant I made sure that she was not worse. She persuaded me that she was okay, and would be better after resting.

She did not know that her "High Self made up her mind to go." According to psychic research, this force of "High Self" made even my mind numb and prevented me from being more alert. I should have grabbed her and run to the Emergency Room. Of course there is no turning back. I should have done that and I should...I should. The Turkish proverb says, *Ecel gelmiş başa başağrısı mana*, which means, *When the appointed hour of death comes, even the headache can be a reason to die.*

The axe came down that afternoon while I was working with Eric in the restaurant; the phone rang and Eric took the call. It was a frantic call from his brother Jim saying that after asking for a glass of water, his mother fell to the floor and couldn't get up. Jim screamed to his grandma to come from downstairs to help him lift his mother.

Jim was in a panic mode and didn't hang up the phone. Repeatedly, I asked him to hang up the phone so I could call the 911. The South Windsor Ambulance responded immediately and they went to the condo. I left work immediately for home and put Eric in charge of the restaurant.

When I arrived home, I found the paramedics applying resuscitation and talking to the doctor at the hospital and following his instructions. She was not responding, and the doctor instructed them to bring her to the hospital.

Carrying her downstairs strapped to the stretcher, Jim in a pleading voice begged "Ba, please bring my mother back." He cried this believing that his father, a survivor of the Turkish boot camp, a fighter strong enough to handle serious problems, could bring his mother back.

Young Jim was now faced with the realities of life. He had to learn bitterly, no matter who we are, when it comes against the Grim Reaper we are like the feather in the wind, helpless and with no ability to change the will of God.

At the hospital the doctor administered more treatment to revive her but nothing helped. I was not only grief-stricken but very angry telling the doctor, "This country sent a man to the moon but can't bring a young person back to life!"

The doctor understood my emotion and took me to his office. There he opened his book of listed patients and expressed his own anguish by saying, "Do you know as a doctor what I am going through? Every day young people die and we don't know why."

ROLLING WITH THE PUNCHES

By now I was calmed down, but still I had to face telling my sons that their mother wouldn't return. It was the Turkish saying, *İçler acısı,* which means, *The pain of the inner souls.*

For me "Time stood still." I went through the motions necessary for taking care of the deceased, with arrangements for her funeral. People came to the wake trying to give me comfort, but I was numb. My lover, friend, soul mate, and support system were gone.

I had two sons and her mother who were going to need me, and I wasn't even able to take care of myself. I was feeling that God had forsaken me, and all the blessings I had from Christians or Muslims were equally worthless.

I remembered "Fuzuli" who said in Turkish, *Şu var sandığın, hani inandığın var sandığın şey yok mu... Yoktur, yok.* In English this means, *The thing you thought exists, well the thing you believed always existed. It doesn't exist, it doesn't exist.* Somehow I went back to Kent Pizza and started taking care of business and my family. For six months customers who had not heard of her death would ask, "Where is your better half?" This was like putting vinegar to the wound.

The pain went on and on. Every morning I had to check the Grandma if she was O.K and while driving to the Restaurant I would ask God, *Why did you take the daughter and leave the mother?* When my sisters insisted on sending my mother-in-law back to Istanbul to her son, I said, "I won't change anything, for maybe God is still testing me." Three years later, I found from my new wife Betty that I was the "Biblical Job."

The young manager of the Sagarino's funeral home gave me the famous book of Harold Kushner—*When Bad Things Happen to Good People.* He then asked me to start life again, and to not be like his father who never stopped grieving the loss of his wife, lamenting for the rest of his life.

Also I found solace in *A Grief Observed* by C.S. Lewis.

CHAPTER IX: My Psychic Research and the Power of Love

I was determined to find out if Ilektra was happy in her new life, and also tried to find answers for my sons who were hurting too.

One of the reasons that made me start a psychic research, even though I was not a believer, was remembering Ilektra's dreams. Every time she would see somebody that we knew with my late mother in her dreams, that person would soon die. A month before she died, she was constantly seeing my mother with my father, which made her ask me, "Why do I see them this time together?" I answered that I didn't know but I thought she shouldn't worry. Later, I found that this was a sign for her departure from this life.

Eric, my older son was grieving quietly as my "Quiet boy." But Jim was a very vocal teenager, angry with God, and not buying any religious explanations.

I remember when our old friends Mr. George and Mrs. Carmenalita Clark came to visit us to console us, she said to me, "You must have done something good in life, and now God is helping you by having the Grandma healthy, helping around the house." I had respect for any belief she had, but Jim, who heard this, jumped to say, "Oh really, God is helping my father? Can you tell me why he did not help my mother?" Everybody in the room was speechless, unable to find an answer.

Like Dr. James Demetriadis (Dean of the Greek Orthodox Cathedral who had also baptized Jim,) spent half an hour trying to persuade him to go back to his activities but had no result.

Observing that nothing seemed to be helping him, a feeling came over me to ask him to pick up his new trombone, which was given to him by his mother. I went on to tell him start the music and read the lives of the great composers, and you may find the healing power of the classical music. He listened, and that was his first step to recovery. He performed in every church and when he asked me what he should perform in his mother's church, the cathedral, I took him again to Dr. James Demetriadis, who had a problem explaining why the Orthodox Church does not allow instruments inside the church during the sermon.

Jim went on working hard with his instrument under George Sanders and music director of South Windsor High, Lou Lazzerini (both members of Hartford Symphony) He involved himself in every musical ensemble he could, including Hartt music school's youth orchestra as well as Boston Symphony's youth orchestra once a week.

His life turned to music, becoming emotionally stronger and experiencing "Subliminal Sonority," and he generally astounded his colleagues and teachers.

It was not long after he won the Hartford Symphony's Young artist competition and in his senior year the prestigious Curtis Music Institute's full scholarship competition.

As I was struggling with my own grief, I was listening to friends and customers who were telling me there are no answers. They said things like, *You are not the first person to suffer or the last, and time will heal you.* I think intellectual people know that time alone won't heal. You have to add a lot of effort of search and activities to the time before it will heal you.

Getting ready for the forty-day memorial in the church, the Greek lady who makes the *Koliva*, a combination of boiled wheat and sugar to be eaten in the memory of the deceased, wanted to comfort me. She said, "The person who dies goes to a better world. For some reason we have to suffer more after them." Hearing her theory it brought to my mind the Turkish theory that says, *Vay gidene*, Pity for the departed, but we are going to make it anyway.

The clash of two different cultures confused me.

More confusion appeared when my priest suggested strongly for me to "Pray."

I tried to pray but I couldn't make it. I told the priest every time I try to pray, when I close my eyes I see the picture of Jim of a few months ago with his hands together praying, or thanking before the dining table to God for having such good parents. I said to the priest if a young innocent boy's prayer was not answered by God, it confuses me to pray.

The priest was taken back with my response, but suggested I try again. Because I remembered and believed in my father's Greek philosophy:

Με το Νου και με την **Γνωση**

Ηυραν τον **Θε**ο καμποσοι

"With the mind and knowledge some people find God."

I decided to go for that destination.

Father James Demetriades
1925 – 2005

"Well done good and faithful servant,
enter into the joy of your Lord."

KNOCKING ON GOD'S DOOR

First, I joined the bereavement groups attended by people of different religions who share the different sufferings and learned the ways of healing. These said that I should not fight the grief, but instead, let this big wave of the ocean go over me and then I would surface in calm water.

In every meeting we had to make a circle, and each person had to explain the different experiences in their grieving. Sometimes at the end of the session we used to make another circle around the person who had a tougher grieving time, like the husband who after losing his first wife, and had now lost his second wife! A mother shared her grief after losing her child and having her other child at the meeting, so as to help him grow stronger.

This experience put my own grief in better perspective. Many nights I would read *The Psychic Mystery* until two or three o'clock in the morning.

I loved the life of "Edgar Cayce" the greatest American Psychic Medium of 1930s who healed so many people. I became member of A.R.E, subscribed to *Fate magazine*, whose main focus was on discovering the secrets of the metaphysical universe, and joined one organization from Washington D.C where the president Ms. Esteep instructed me for some experiments and the art of communicating with those on the other side.

I did not successfully receive a message from the other side. But Ms. Esteep insisted I should continue, telling me, "Keep trying. You will definitely receive a message, perhaps from a different avenue." She was right. One morning as I was driving to the cemetery before going to work, I had the radio on which was playing a beautiful song. The singer had a very dramatic voice.

On leaving the cemetery I turned to another favorite station of mine which was playing the same song. When I was operating in the restaurant, the first customer happened to select in the jukebox that same song. At this point I went over to the jukebox to find the name of the song, which was, "The Power of Love." It wasn't too long after that, that another customer came in and while she was waiting for her order to be prepared, she selected the same song in the jukebox.

This time I decided to find out what the lyrics were and I assigned my worker (a high school senior) to write down the words the best he could by listening over and over. When I read the lyrics, I was stunned by what I was reading, and I knew this was a message from Ilektra!

The music and the constant wailing of the singer roused me into a state of guilt. Gradually I came out of my guilt and realized that the message actually was to let me know how much she loved me. A particular stanza from the song left a heart-stirring imprint on my inner soul:

Whenever you reach for me, I'll do all that I can,
Even though there may be times I seem so far away.
Don't ever wonder where I am, cause I am always
**   by your side,**
Cause I'm your lady and you are my man.
Sometimes I am frightened, but I'm ready to run
about the POWER of LOVE.

The customers who had become friendly with me took great interest in my grief and were trying to help me. One of the couples, Frank and Roberta, who were members of a Spiritual Church, wanted me to meet their spiritual leader Reverend Margiada. So arrangements were made for me to meet for the first time a real medium in Waterbury.

As I sat in her living room, the door opened and she entered in a wheelchair pushed by her attendant. She lifted her arm and pointed at me saying, "You young man; you have to take care of that old lady who is living with you for quite awhile." She then gave me a reading and advised me to try to be happy again because that would make my deceased wife happy also.

When my mother-in-law died three and half years later, my sons remembered the prediction and said, "We thought she was going to live for a long time; how come she died so soon? My response was, "It may not seem long time for you but for me it has been long."

Because I never complained, they did not realize how taking care of her needs drained me. One of my efforts was to make sure she had enough yarn for knitting, so she could stay busy. Since she was a professional knitter, she frequently ran out of the yarn, which made me run repeatedly to KMART, where the sales girls grew to know me and invariably would greet me saying: "Is grandma out of yarn again?"

After awhile, we had so many sweaters that I did not know what to do. I decided to take all of them to a meeting of bereavement group and give away as Christmas gifts. The women were very happy and wanted to thank her and wish Grandma a Happy New Year. One of the ladies wanted to know if she could order an afghan for her granddaughter. When I approached my mother-in-law with the request, she balked by saying, "I can't do that; I only knit sweaters."

I tried to persuade her but my efforts were in vain. When she said, "I know why I am suffering and don't make it worst." I responded, "I know you are suffering, but you are not alone; your grandchildren and I are suffering as well."

I went on to say that sometimes we are not happy with the work for which we are responsible but we have to carry on because it is God's order and not my order to you, so please try to do this work.

After leaving her with this message, it was not long before she began knitting the afghan. As I delivered the completed afghan to the lady, I explained to her how I had to use this inspiration, which I felt had come from God.

With time Grandma grew weaker. One morning when I went to check on her I found her unable to get out from bed, so I carried her upstairs to the living room and placed her on the couch. Later her situation worsened and she had to be hospitalized, where they discovered she had pancreatic cancer which we knew was a serious illness.

My older son Eric remembered that we did not have the chance to call the priest for his mother, and we should have him there for his grandma. I said, "She may not like to see the priest but I will do what you say." My instinct was correct, because when the priest showed up she whispered to me in Albanian, "Why did you call him?"

Obviously some people are never ready for the other world.

Reflecting on my experience with psychics, I admit I went to a few who were frauds. When I sensed that they were giving me pseudo information, I would end the session. In sharing this experience with Frank (who himself and his wife belonged to the Spiritual Church) he suggested that his wife can help because she has shown excellent ability to give readings.

THE PSYCHIC PHENOMENA

The arrangements were made for a session and it was really an astonishing experience in psychic phenomena.

As I sat there, his wife fell into a trance and started saying/conveying with a master angel named Martina, who was watching over Ilektra (my wife). From the name Martina, which is a cognate of Martira, I found that she is my mother. She continued telling me the names of my father, two uncles, aunt and a young cousin whose name was "Iris." She informed me that they were around me and they share my pain, wanting to tell me how much they loved me. "I am convinced that we have to understand as the images of the deceased people come to psychics and they introduce themselves, their names may be slightly different than the originals, like Martina-Martira, Michael-Mihalis, Iris-Ritsa, who is the mother of my cousin Sofula Barshan."

This reading was real, because she could not have known this information since the ones she mentioned were all from Istanbul, Turkey. She would have had to know Turkish or Greek.

In the meantime, candid customers were giving me meaningful supportive advice such as, "We know that you are a capable strong man and we want you to roll with the punches." Another customer (a female) advised me, "You have to stop grieving, because you have to make another lady happy."

My good friends Warren and Barbara of Tolland who knew Ilektra wanted to help me by inviting a minister and me to their home for prayer and healing. I considered this a very compassionate gesture. Furthermore, Warren gave me philosophical advice: "We know that everything you worked so hard for is now in the ashes, but you have to rise again like the Bird of Phoenix from the ashes."

Lastly, Warren and Barbara indicated that they were inviting Dr. Ricci (Author and Head of the Evangelical Ministry), who they believed would help me in my suffering and healing and answering all my questions. Within this meeting I would definitely be motivated to start a new life.

As usual, I wanted first to read Dr. Ricci's book and get his ideas, from the sermons he did about healing after suffering in life.

When we met in my friend's house, I had my notes and tough questions for him such as "Can you show me any proof of your teachings that can lead me to a better understanding of Life, Faith, and Death? After so many centuries of different religions not guiding us to Utopia, what makes you think your denomination is the best?

After an hour of conversational debate, Dr. Ricci terminated the discussion by saying, "I am unable to answer any further questions because of your background, religion, and suffering."

My friends, Warren and Barbara were disappointed and upset at the outcome of our meeting. They scolded me by saying, "What is the matter? Why were you not satisfied with his advice?"

I replied, "Because I have a reason."

They said, "Come on. What reason? Be understandable."

Dr. Ricci interfered by asking me, "What is the reason, Anesti?"

My response was that after centuries of human history and education, if we can't find an answer for our kids, we have to study harder to find God. To my surprise, Dr. Ricci agreed with my point of view.

We sat down at the table for the dinner, when a lady who was Dr. Ricci's wife chose to sit next to me. As people took their places she turned to me saying "With your attitude and perseverance I can see that, now, God is next to you." Automatically without thinking I looked around me and suddenly I felt an enlightenment which continued through the evening.

Shortly afterward I met my present wife, Betty.

CHAPTER X: A New Beginning

I had been widowed about three years and I decided to exit my grief and seek joy by attending some social functions. I also became aware that if you help someone, you are also helping yourself.

In the coming days I was told that one of my male customers had lost his wife and was having a difficult time dealing with his grief. Without hesitation I wanted to help him. I heard that the Congregational Church on Tolland Green was conducting meetings once a week for singles—the never married, divorced and widowed. Because he knew about this church, I suggested that we go to one of those meetings.

Like my friend I was still hurting, but I knew I had to move on, so together we went. It really was an interesting time. Fun activities were planned so that those gathered would have a chance to relax and have fun with other singles.

The minister in charge of forming this group was Hannah Howe. She herself had been widowed and after seven years, met her second husband.

They did not meet through such a group, but her time alone made her aware that safe havens are important for singles. Likewise the social director of our group was a woman who had been widowed about four years.

She had worked her way through her grief process by herself and never felt the need for a social group. However, she had a great respect for Hannah and wanted to help facilitate the group to a successful outcome. I have since been told that after that meeting in Feb. 1992, she and Hannah were cleaning the area before heading home. It seems that in a conversation Hannah asked her friend, "Have you met the man from Kent Pizza?" She replied, "I don't know him." Hannah went on to tell her what a nice man he was, so this lady decided that if God opened a door, the least one could do is to peek in. She did more than that.

The next day she came to the pizzeria and bought a pizza. While the pizza was baking, she read the article about the Novas, which Steve Jensen had written for the Hartford Courant the previous fall with the title, "Classical Music Plays Key Note For Family."

Little did I know that she was to be my second wife. Our relationship started slowly. I continued to attend some meetings, but when the Pizza business kept me away from a meeting, some of the group would stop by the Pizzeria with this lady. She sensed my need to socialize, and would invite me to accompany her to different social activities.

There were times when she would stop by the restaurant to just talk. Our conversation often was about our widowhood and sharing about our spouses.

It didn't take much for my tears to flow; she seemed so strong and comfortable even though she was sitting across the table from a teary-eyed man. She has since told me that she was drawn to me. I am not sure I remember a lot about those chance meetings, but I do know this lady was determined not to go away. When I closed my restaurant at the end of the day, I invited her out to dinner.

Later, if I wanted to leave work at an earlier time so as to meet this lady for our "Chat and chew," Eric, my older son would "Hold down the fort." As our relationship grew, she would come and help me in the restaurant. Together we called it, "Working in the backroom."

The fourth of July was coming and she invited me and my sons to join her family for the day because a big wedding reception was being held in the backyard of her home. Her oldest son had been married the previous week in a private service, so this was a time to celebrate with relatives.

As I walked into the backyard with my sons, I saw tables and chairs under a large canopy already occupied by her relatives and a group of Dale's friends. She greeted me with a flare and took me table to table introducing me as her special friend.

While my sons played volleyball and other games, Jim my younger son, observed this lady staying so close to me. At the end of the reception he asked me directly, " Is this lady going to replace my mother?" I guess I had anticipated this, for I came out with the answer, "No one can replace your mother, but I need help to go on with life." He quickly replied, "Sorry for that question; it was just the kid inside me coming out."

On July fifth Betty, my future wife flew to Athens to join a tour group which was visiting archeological sites. This tour was planned and paid for before our first date. It so happened that my two sisters lived in Athens and when they learned of her visit there, arrangements were made to meet my special friend. At this point I rather wanted their input. My younger sister's friend spoke fluent English so she was the translator and it proved to be a very positive experience.

Before Betty came home I had a conversation with my sisters about our friendship, which set the stage for the possibility of a permanent relationship.

The tour on which she traveled ended in Istanbul where she met my Muslim veteran friend, Ismail, of the Turkish Army Band (the heavy B flat Sousaphone player) who ran a bookstore in the Grand Bazaar, specializing in finding the right books for the professors of University.

She was a (gutsy) brave lady; she even accepted an invitation to visit his summer home on Heybeli, an island, where she met his wife and two daughters. At that time Ismail had a worker who was Buddhist and spoke English. Because he could be their interpreter, he was invited to accompany them on the ferry and dinner. During this social event Ismail showed to her the summer house we used to have at the same island when we were in Istanbul.

I am sure Betty was the first American lady to impress his wife and daughters. She was like an ambassador of the American goodwill. When she thanked Ismail for his hospitality and friendliness, he replied, "Don't mention it because Anesti is my brother."

My veteran friend Ismail Akçay after 40 years

When Betty returned, we were like a perfect couple. She had a strong faith and we were both convinced that God was our matchmaker, unlike the matchmaker of my first marriage who was my mother. Consequently I asked her on Christmas Eve to marry me.

THE DOGMA

In the meantime, I had a conversation with my priest, Dr. James Demetriadis, who told me: "If you are going to your special friend's church to receive communion, we have to excommunicate you from the Greek Orthodox Church."

I said, "I thought these excommunications only existed in Medieval Europe and not here in America (Land of the free and home of the brave.).

He replied, " I know and I understand you but we have the Dogma, and Archiepiscopy (Archbishop) orders us to excommunicate those who stray."

I had to tell my sons the existing situation, but when Betty heard this, she told me "Don't get in trouble. I will come to your church to marry you."

Arrangements were made for our wedding to be held at the Greek Orthodox Cathedral of Hartford Jan. 17, 1993.

Knowing the Greek Ceremony lasts for an hour, I asked the priest to give us the shortest version he could. Because we were widowed, we chose to keep things simple, with only the immediate family and a few friends `attending.

My son, Eric, was my best man and Betty's maid of honor was Suzie Ghantous who six months later became her daughter-in-law.

I made sure that my priest would allow Betty's clergymen, Reverend Don Miller, Reverend Joseph Zezo and Reverend Hannah Howe to be present and give us prayers. When their turn came to approach the altar, my priest whispered to me, "Don't let her (Hannah) come to the altar; women are not allowed there." I quickly told her, "Please don't come to the altar. Say your prayer from there."

After the ceremony the priest spoke apologetically for the inconvenience, explaining the "Dogma." The explanation was accepted, and together we went to the reception.

A few weeks later we went to the church to obtain our marriage certificate from the priest. When examining, it revealed this was my second marriage to Betty; however, under her name was written first marriage to Anesti Nova. We informed the priest of a mistake in the certificate, he replied, "The Archiepiscopy (Archbishop) doesn't recognize the non-Orthodox marriage."

While I was thinking how they do this in America, Betty, who had three adult sons from her first marriage, instinctively spoke up and said, "Oh, I have three bastards running around." The priest said, "Oh, please don't say that."

It was so embarrassing seeing my wife be put in this situation, but her humor revealed how ridiculous the rules of my religion were.

Shortly after, I had a conversation about these events with Reverend Hannah. I told her how I felt was critical and causing trouble, and how I felt I was not that religious. She complimented me saying, "You are more religious than what you think you are."

When formerly married people who have been widowed come together as Betty and I did, ideally they would leave their houses and move to a new place. Because Betty knew that my two sons were still living with me, and did not want them to be uprooted, she chose to move from her nine-room furnished house to my five-room furnished condo.

Her sensitivity as a mother and a retired teacher made her aware that what is really important are people and things will have to take second place. However, she did make a few changes at the condo to make it her home too.

A combined family after our marriage

LOSING A MENTOR

Eric, continued to help at the restaurant while he pursued his studies in engineering at Univ. of Conn. One evening at the condo Betty had a conversation with Eric who opened up to her about how much he missed his mother, grandmother, and felt nobody understood his feelings.

The conversation shifted to his education, and he told Betty how difficult it was to deal with constant changing standards in engineering. Furthermore, he had lost the guidance of his mentor, Prof. Hayrettin Kardeştuncer, a highly respected figure in engineering department and a guiding instructor in Ankara-Turkey his homeland.

He was a very nice man and helped Eric; unfortunately, he suffered a stroke and was out of commission. Eric told Betty that he wanted to transfer to Central University of Connecticut where he would continue studying engineering, but he was afraid to tell me.

Betty took over, telling him, "Now it is time for you to make the decision in what *you* want to do. I will talk to your father." So with Betty's help, Eric was able to transfer to Central Connecticut.

Her help as a stepmother—but actually being more like a real friend and mentor—must have touched the spiritual world, for one morning she related a dream to me about a woman thanking her for what she had done for her son. Describing the woman who invited her to have a drink together in the dream, made me believe it was Ilektra.

The following year Eric graduated from Central as a civil engineer while on weekends still helping in the restaurant.

Like Eric, my younger son Jim graduated two years later from Curtis Music Institute and went to Boston for his masters and studied in the New England Conservatory under professor and composer Norman Bolton who opened the door for him to become a member of the Boston Pops.

Jim's mentor and instructor Prof. Norman Bolter

THE FIRE

One evening in December 1994, after the restaurant was closed, a fire occurred during the night. Sometime after midnight I went to examine the damage; however, the fire chief did not permit me to enter the building due to policy rules and regulations. Only the town's fire marshal had to investigate and file his report, which was, *Not arson.* However, the owners of Cumberland Farms property summoned another fire marshal to reexamine the site, his findings negated the original report and indicated that the cause of the fire was arson. A third fire marshal from the state was contacted, who after his investigation also stated that the fire was not arson. He claimed the fire started because the shingles above the ovens were overheated and caught fire.

When I entered the restaurant, I found it was really damaged. I found also a spot that made me suspicious about the fire. Fortunately I had a good insurance policy, which enabled me to rebuild the business in another location across the street in the new plaza.

EMINENT DOMAIN AND THE SMALL BUSINESS

Meanwhile, I was attempting to buy the property of Cumberland Farms, which, somehow the town of Tolland took by right of "Eminent Domain" and gave to the Fire department of Tolland.

In eight months with my wife's help I was able to open a brand new restaurant with a wider menu. I had to fight the famous health inspector of the town who was giving me a hard time during the construction of the restaurant, by adding new requirements every time he saw me.

After concentrating on a strategy, one early morning I had with me the architect who designed the interior of the restaurant and my lawyer to make a surprise visit to the health inspector, who could not move any more to give his word to my lawyer that he doesn't have any more excuses to forestall the opening.

In spite of this, he still tried to keep me from opening by not signing the occupation paper. At this point my patience was exhausted, like the Turkish saying, "The knife this time came to the bone." In Turkish that would be, *Bıçak kemiğe dayandı.* So I let him know in no uncertain terms I was going to open with or without his permission. Seeing my determination, he finally signed the conditional certificate with the understanding that he would return in fifteen days.

He did not show up again. I think he got the message that he can't fool around with a Turkish Army veteran!

The recently married couple managing a new restaurant in Tolland

CHAPTER XI: Goodbye Restaurant, Hello Music

I knew from the very moment we opened the new restaurant, Nova Pizza and Family Restaurant, that I would be selling it within a year or two. Betty was a retired Home Economics teacher. She was helping me at the restaurant, but had had a taste of freedom from a career and wanted me to have the same opportunity.

I had made a promise to her that after getting the business back on track, I would sell it. She knew I had to rebuild after the fire. Her sensitivity to my losing all that my late wife and I had work for, would leave a negative blot on my life. In spite of my misfortune, she really wanted me to "Hang it up." However, she relented and supported my desire to rebuild.

Within a year, business was back to normal. Old customers were excited to once again enjoy their favorite food and dine in a new place, which was decorated by Betty. I felt like she had also decorated my life, like Kenny Roger's song.

Within this context the music, philosophy, world events and topics of general interest were discussed. Needless to say I was back in my element, but Betty with all her great ways of dealing with people, still yearned for retirement. Again the words of "Hang It Up," rang clearly in my ears.

Reflecting on this advice, I realized the journey of life gives us many choices. Retirement is one thing many people seldom have the opportunity to enjoy. Both my wife and I decided my time had come to retire and enjoy the fruits of my labor. Wisdom of the ages provides one with encouragement:

"When One Door Closes, Another Door Will Open." For me, the open door gave me the time to resume my interest in music.

We had been open for almost two years, when suddenly a buyer came along. He seemed sincere in wanting to take over the business. After making sure he understood that he would be successful if he ran it as a family, he assured me he would. I agreed to the sale, signed papers and started the life of a retired man, actually retiring to a new life.

With this new freedom, we traveled, but gradually, I was drawn to my music. I began practicing the accordion, recording myself for the classical pieces that I was dreaming of twenty years before. During my practice with the accordion melodies would come to me. My harmonies were simple at first, but I had the desire to orchestrate them. I had studied composition in Germany years ago, and felt I needed to brush up, so I went to a bookstore and purchased a book for orchestration.

My son Jim, who is a professional musician, advised me to take courses at Hartt School of Music to enhance my musical skills.

I connected with Dr. Steve Gryc who encouraged me to study orchestration after listening to my "Valse Triste" for the 9/11 tragedy. He became my private instructor. Also, Prof. Ken Steen made it possible for me to start learning how to use the computer to transcribe the notation for orchestra. With their help, four of my pieces were ready for performance.

With their blessings, I searched for endowments to fund an orchestra to play my compositions. After a year, I knew this was not going to happen.

Even my own culture's endowment of the Archiepiscopy for talented music students and their Greek Orchestra in New York would not help Jim who had already became principal trombonist for the Boston Pops Esplanade.

A DREAM COME TRUE

Again, Hartt came through, one of the professors suggested that I contact Dr. Harry in Canada who coordinated work contacts with European orchestras for composers in Canada and the U.S. I sent him a copy of the pieces I wanted recorded. On checking the music, he said he had the perfect orchestra for me, which was the Symphonika Bulgarika in Sofia Bulgaria.

I agreed to his suggestion, and on February 2004, Jim and I left for Sofia, Bulgaria. All of the compositions I had written for the orchestra had the trombone as the solo instrument, and the Albanian Rhapsody with Trombone Obligato. It was interesting when the maestro of the orchestra asked me if the soloist is good enough to accomplish the recording with the orchestra in the scheduled time? I said, "I know he is good because he is my son, but you have to find if he is good enough for your orchestra."

From the other side, my son Jim, who had never been in Europe, asked me if those Bulgarian musicians are as good as the Americans? I replied, "You are going to find out if they are good enough for us."

This family venture in believing and going for a dream with God's help made us find the unexpected memorable and outstanding experience in the world of music where there are no borders or politics.

In the first rehearsal those Bulgarian musicians who were trained in Russian classical discipline with their Maestro, Valery Vatchev (Vienna graduated) started working with Jim with great enthusiasm. Jim was surprised with their competence and told me, "Ba, those guys are great. I think they'll make a fine recording."

They were also motivated with my asking the maestro for a "brotherly help" based in what my father used to tell me. I said, "Once upon a time we were all brothers in Balkans, and I will take the orchestra and you to dinner after the job is finished." I said this to him instinctively, without thinking, which was my father's tradition. I was scolded by my son and my wife who said this is very expensive to take the whole orchestra to dinner.

But their effort in working meticulously to interpret my music in "Balkanic" spirit was much more important than the money. It was nice to see my son, an America born performer, get the experience of the Balkan camaraderie of his ancestors and hugging each other in the universal language of music which reaches into eternity.

Jim introduced his own cadenza in five octaves for the Trombone Concerto (written for his mother) to express his depression and pain in losing his mother. The orchestra actually had two conductors, and the second maestro, Christo Christov. Working with the other maestro, in the recording studio, he produced a quality recording.

GOD-INCIDENT

When unusual things happen in a person's life, it is often referred to as a coincidence, but Betty and I like to think of this as "God-incidents." It was two of these experiences that made us aware of the spirits.

First, in the third part of the concerto, one of the dances was stopped by Maestro Christov, who wanted the orchestra to play it in a different style because "Çorbacı" will dance. Çorbacı is a Turkish term for the respected people or leaders who lead the dance. This term was established during the Ottoman Empire. The Turks in Istanbul used to call my father, "Çorbacı."

After dinner, my father's portrait appeared a second time when some of the orchestra members started playing their folk dances with their violins. A senior musician danced like my father with his handkerchief while some of them called out

Hayde Koço the same call, the Greeks, Albanians used to call my father in Istanbul.

The whole evening was a memorable experience. Incidentally, much to Betty's relief, the restaurateur who heard my story charged only $500.00 for the members of the orchestra!

**Turning back from Bulgaria we visited Jim's
favorite uncle, aunts and cousins in Athens**

We returned to America elated with our experience. The finished recording was sent to us within two months and arrangements were made with Summit studios to make a CD for the market. The Albanian Rhapsody can be purchased at Borders and other music stores.

Meanwhile, our family nest was further blessed. Eric, my older son married Entela who had been a teacher in Albania and immigrated to Boston. This marriage came about through what I call, "A Modern Matchmaking Event." It happened when a large number of Albanians in the 1990's immigrated to Boston. Among them were Entela's parents and my cousin, Taso, whose wife Ela knew Entela, and who introduced her to Eric.

The match was perfect and the marriage angelic. Entela was baptized at the Albanian Orthodox Church and soon after was married to Eric at the Greek Orthodox Church in Boston. After the traditional Orthodox ceremony, a very lovely reception was held at the Peer Fort restaurant, which overlooks the Boston Harbor. Entela's father, Shpetimi, is a chef in this restaurant.

All the guests enjoyed the food and listened and danced to the melodic rhythms of Albanian and Greek music.

They settled in Boston, where Eric is a civil engineer and Entela is employed as a coordinator in South Boston Medical Center. In 2005 they had a daughter whom they named Olivia Ilektra.

In 2006 the Historical Society of Hartford put together a presentation in honor of the people who died in the 9/11 2001 tragedy and they chose my music "Valse Triste" for this event. I was inspired to write this music by feeling the pain of the father and mother in New York who had to attend a funeral instead of a wedding for their daughter who was traveling on the plane that hit the tower.

Thank God my son Jim was spared by not taking that particular flight that day, since he used to take it regularly for concerts and auditions.

Since then, Jim started believing in "Protective Angels." Every year the 9/11 Tragedy Memorial is documented in a different town of Connecticut.

The premier of three of my works was played at the International Trombone Festival in Salt Lake City in 2008. It was with great pride that my music was played in America with my son Jim, as the trombone soloist with the Utah Symphony conducted by Robert Baldwin.

The warmth of the conductor, concertmeister, the players and friends who helped this dream come true in Salt Lake City was memorable. However, there's been no concert in my own city. My wife says, "A prophet is not without honor except in his own country."

Another happy event occurred in the Nova Family. My younger son Jim, when he became a member of Utah Symphony met Lindsey, a musician who is a singer and who plays the French horn. Lindsey later became director of operations of the Utah Symphony. After a few years courtship, they chose to be married in a very romantic French Villa called "La Caille," located in Little Cottonwood Canyon in Salt Lake City.

My sister, Christine, who came all the way from Athens Greece for the wedding, is multi-linguistic like me. Knowing very little English, she enjoyed speaking French fluently with Lindsey who taught English in a small town in France for a year. She also spoke Greek to Jim.

We experienced the triumph of music that connects different culture's young people to the happiness of marriage. Jim and Lindsey had both lost their mothers, and this was another bond to bring them together.

Jim's friends formed a trombone ensemble, which performed for half an hour prior to the ceremony, where a nondenominational minister performed the ceremony.

In front of the area where the ceremony was to take place, there were two empty chairs facing the attendees. Jim and Lindsey stood between the empty chairs which represented their mothers who had passed away.

In the beginning of the ceremony Eric (Jim's brother) gave Jim a bouquet of red roses, and David (Lindsey's brother) gave Lindsey a bouquet of yellow roses, their mother's favorite flowers. Each placed their bouquet on the vacant chairs in honor of their mothers.

This tribute was beautiful and very emotional for many attendees. Later, Jim performed Ravel's "Pavane for a Dead Princess" with the trombone ensemble, symbolic of their mothers. With a small jazz combo, he also performed the classic jazz ballad, Tommy Dorsey's, "I'm Getting Sentimental for you." Then Lindsey surprised Jim by singing "At Last" with the jazz combo.

LAST THOUGHT AND THE ROAD

As a musician and a lover of art and history, I hope that American readers will see the beauty and good qualities of other cultures. If you support art and music and diversity, you will help promote peace in this very troubled world. We must see the good things in people, even if they are from a different culture. As Shakespeare's Juliet said, "What is in a name? That which we call a rose by any other name would smell as sweet." The winding road of life took me from one world to another. I have made many friends, faced adversity and experienced joy. God blessed me with two great marriages and a wonderful extended family. Yes, I'm a lucky man. The road continues—when life calls, I'll be ready.

CPSIA information can be obtained at www.ICGtesting.com
Printed in the USA
BVOW02s1153221013

334301BV00007B/95/P

9 781609 100650